Teas of the World

Other Books by
NANCY HYDEN WOODWARD

The Mariner's Cookbook
The Food Catalogue
Vacation!

TEAS
of the
WORLD

Nancy Hyden Woodward

COLLIER BOOKS

A Division of Macmillan Publishing Co., Inc.

NEW YORK

COLLIER MACMILLAN PUBLISHERS

LONDON

Macmillan Publishing Co., Inc.
866 Third Avenue, New York, N.Y. 10022
Collier Macmillan Canada, Ltd.

Library of Congress Cataloging in Publication Data
Woodward, Nancy Hyden.
Teas of the world.
Includes index.
1. Tea.   I. Title.
TX415.W66   641.3′372   80-17441
ISBN 0-02-082870-5

10   9   8   7   6   5   4   3   2   1

The lines from Dylan Thomas, *Under Milkwood*, copyright
1954 by New Directions Publishing Corporation. Reprinted
by permission of New Directions.

Printed in the United States of America

BOOK DESIGN BY RON FARBER

For
NANNY (Ethel E. Green)
. . . *and for*
TEE ADAMS

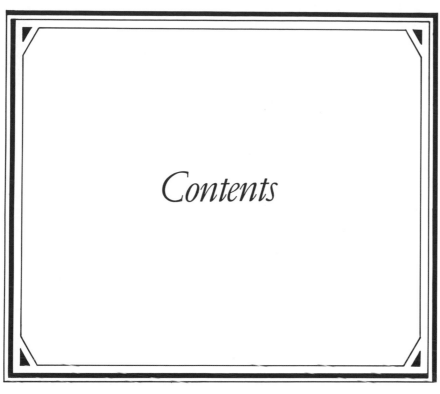

Contents

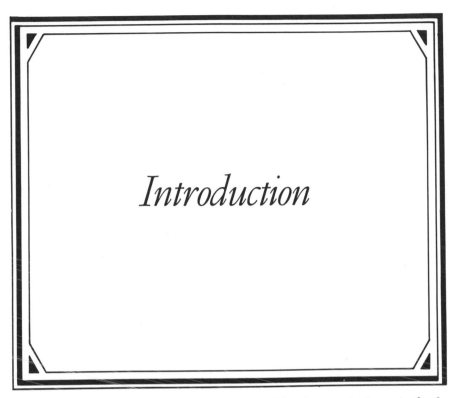

Introduction

IT MIGHT BE CONSIDERED presumptuous to claim that tea is the only food or beverage to have made an indelible mark on our eating and drinking habits. One only has to mention pizza, coffee and peanut butter as examples. But it can be safely said that of all foods, solid or liquid, tea has had the most extraordinary influence down the centuries and around the globe.

It has played a part in history, medicine, currency, politics, naval architecture, literature, manners and fashion. Even in the illicit rendezvous. Yet the number of uses for which tea has been employed almost could be topped by the number of references alluding to its origin. The imagination, if not the reality, is positively dazzling.

That tea survived at all in the Western world is a miracle, considering the verbal assaults leveled against its introduction first to the European continent and then to England. At one point tea was a veritable cause célèbre. But for every attacker two enthusiasts rose in its favor, champions to the last leaf.

The drinking of tea has served as more than an opportunity to visit with friends and family or to engage in relationships "more meaningful." Tea has been a source of inspiration for the religious and the carefree, for the painter, writer, politician and master artisan since its discovery. It has evoked all manner of packaging and presentation, from the utilitarian to the most supreme of designs. And it has been celebrated with humor, fervor and purpose in books, poetry, painting, sculpture and music.

Perhaps the pleasures of tea can best be summed up by England's Sidney Smith, an eighteenth-century clergyman and author known more for his impeccable wit than for his ecclesiastical contributions. Also famous for his London breakfasts and dinners, in tea he found solace and refreshment, and a cup was always near at hand to the man who said:

> Thank God for tea! What would the world do without tea? How did it exist? I am glad I was not born before tea.

The leading Fair the Word harmonious gives;
  Betty around attends with bending Knee.
Each white-arm Fair, the painted Cup receives;
  Pours the rich Cream, or stirs the sweetened Tea.

ANONYMOUS, "Tea Drinking; a Fragment" (c. 1752)

1

The Beginnings of Tea

Tell me, gypsy, what can you see
in my cup of tea?
Can you predict my future,
tell me my past?

ANONYMOUS

OF ONE FACT the tea world is certain: the gypsy could no more authenticate the beginnings of tea than historians and fabulists. The origin of tea has been blessed with as many theories as those accorded Stonehenge and the monolithic heads on Easter Island. Centuries pass, new hypotheses are put forth, but the puzzle remains, truth woven into a gloriously aged tapestry of fables and legends, some colored with a certain nobility, others plainly outlandish.

LEGENDS

Leaf through recorded history and one date keeps coming up—2737 B.C.—the legendary year pinpointing the discovery of tea. And the discoverer? Shen Nung, the Chinese emperor born to a beautiful young princess while she was possessed by a heavenly dragon, and who was known as the Divine Healer, the Divine Husbandman, and the Divine Cultivator. Shen Nung himself was the product of a richly spun lineage that began with the separation of Earth and Heaven giving birth to the world. The new universe was governed first by the twelve Emperors of Heaven, each of whom reigned for eighteen thousand years, followed by the eleven Emperors of Earth who also managed to rule for eighteen thousand years each. They were succeeded by nine Emperors of Mankind whose combined sovereignty totaled a little over forty-five thousand years and then by sixteen Emperors whose biographies and accomplishments remain an extraordinary blank. The sixteen unknowns preceded the Three Sovereigns Lu Hsi, Huang Ti, and Shen Nung. All of them lived south of the Yellow River in the province of Hunan, and they originated all of the world's arts and crafts. Shen Nung, whose name means Spirit of the Land, also tilled the soil.

How then did he come upon tea? Legend pictures Shen Nung a hygienist, greatly concerned with cleanliness and purity, to the point that he boiled his drinking water daily. One day leaves from a branch burning under the pot were caught by the wind and tossed into the churning pot. A marvelous aroma overtook Shen Nung, who was standing nearby, and he sniffed the pot carefully. He liked what his nostrils took in and tasted some of the water as soon as it cooled. The entire experience was so pleasurable to Shen Nung that he immediately sought out more branches of the same quality, pointed them out to his subjects and suggested that they be cultivated with care. The branches came from the tea tree whose formal name today is *Camellia sinensis*.

You may go to Carlisle's, and to Almack's too;
And I'll give you my head if you find such a host,
For coffee, tea, chocolate, butter and toast;
How he welcomes at once all the world and his wife,
And how civil to folks he ne'er saw in his life.

CHRISTOPHER ANSTEY (1724–1805)
The New Bath Guide, letter 13, "A Public Benefactor"

Indian myth, on the other hand, clings to the theory that the Buddhist worthy Bodhidharma, who really did live and who founded the Ch'an (Zen in Japan) School of Buddhism, discovered tea. Bodhidharma, also known as Daruma, left India for China where he took up contemplative residence in a cave-temple cut into the mountains lying just beyond the capital of Nanking and offered to him by Emperor Lian Wu Ti. Daruma planned to meditate nine years, seated the entire time facing one wall. All went well the first four years—a feat which led the impressed Chinese to dub him *Tamo* or *White Buddha*. But even White Buddhas can tire, and into his fifth year drowsiness intruded, breaking his concentration and finally taking hold. Almost unconsciously Daruma reached for some nearby twigs, snapped them off the branch and began chewing on them. Within moments he was wide awake, alert and ready to continue his divine contemplation to its conclusion with, one might say, barely the bat of an eyelash. The miracle twigs of course belonged to the until then unknown tea tree. The year was A.D. 527.

For the most part the Japanese agreed with this tired tale, and the Buddhists of Japan delighted in promoting the legend far and wide. But their particular version was outrageous. They claimed that when sleep overcame Daruma and he realized what had happened, he was so mortified that he cut off his eyelids and hurled them to the ground to make certain it could never happen again. Within moments a pair of tea plants sprang from the soil in place of his eyelids.

"Oh, my friends, be warned by me,
That breakfast, dinner, lunch and tea
Are all the human frame requires...."
With that the wretched child expires.

HILAIRE BELLOC (1870–1953), *Cautionary Tales, Henry King*

But did tea's first roots take hold in China soil? Or was it somewhere else? And when did China first know tea as a drink? No one questions that tea as an industry began in China. But the belief has been held that the plant actually originated in fine form in India and was introduced in less fine form (smaller leaf, less robust) to China. Supporting this thesis is the legend of Gan Lu which, understandably, has never been included in any major work on tea published in China.

The legend suggests that the Buddhist scholar Gan Lu, who lived during the Later Han dynasty (A.D. 25–221), returned from studying in India bearing seven tea plants which he rooted on Meng Mountain in the province of Szechwan. It has been said by students of the Orient that the first cultivation of the tea plant took place in Szechwan, but even that has been subject to question. In China today there is proof offered from the centuries-old records kept on tea that tea began in Yunan Province and was introduced from there into central China where the leaf changed style.

As might be guessed, trying to document the origin of tea is not an easy task. Early historians and botanists found themselves deciphering pages of Chinese history overlaid with a fine web of fantasy. The web was spun on order of emperors seeking to improve their image or to make a point. When the royal scribes began recording the historical folklore that had been handed down orally for years, the emperors took advantage of the transition. History was ordered rewritten in part or in whole, with segments left out and others juggled. Credit was taken for events that never occurred during an emperor's reign and failings or defeat were attributed to predecessors to whom they were not due. In short, history was manipulated with a fine flair and large ego.

The warping of China's heritage began in the third century B.C. during the Ch'in dynasty (220–207 B.C.) of Shih-Hwang-ti, under whom China was unified for the first time. After conquering the warring feudal states that periodically rose and fell during the earlier Chou dynasty, Shih-Hwang-ti ordered their political, social and cultural systems destroyed. With feudalism abolished as a way of life, he then ordered every trace of it erased from the books. He also ordered the burning of every philosophical work, especially the writings of Confucius.

Hail Queen of Plants, Pride of Elysian Bowers!!
How shall we speak thy complicated Pow'rs?
Thou Wond'rous Panacea to asswage
The Calentures of Youth's fermenting rage,
And Animate the freezing Veins of age.

Thus our Tea-Conversation we employ
Where with Delight; Instruction we enjoy;
Quaffing, without the waste of Time or Wealth,
The Sov'reign Drink of Pleasure and of Health.

NICHOLAS BRADY (1659–1726), "The Tea Table," Stanzas 1 and 4

During the Early Han period that followed almost immediately (202 B.C.–A.D. 22), the past was resurrected as the foundation of the present. Confucianism became the basis for the state and history was gradually reclaimed through the fragments of writings that survived the flames. Here too history was ill-served by "well-meaning" emperors. In trying to give the past greater significance, Han emperors ended by creating a montage of history. They decided which parts of history would be put down on paper again. Some episodes were blown up to twice their importance and certain myths were written into history. Legends became reality and the truth, further stretched and somewhat smothered, tumbled in between. The original route to tea's origins became even further obscured. Credit for its discovery was claimed by or given to different people in different times.

Those who believed that the first seeds of the tea plant nurtured in China's soil held up the *Pen ts'ao* as proof. The medical book, they claimed, was written by Shen Nung, who discovered tea and wrote about it in the passage: "Bitter *t'u* is called *ch'a*, *hsuan* and *yu*. It grows in the valleys and streams and on the hills of Ichow (in Szechwan Province) and does not perish in severe winter." *T'u*, according to the *Pen ts'ao*, could wither tumors and abscesses of the head; cure bladder, lung and chest infections; quench thirst and ward off sleep. It could even make one happy. It would seem that *t'u* was a veritable panacea.

For further proof *China First* advocates offered quotes from *Shih Ching*, the Book of Songs, edited by Confucius around 550 B.C. Ode Ten, "The

Lament of a Discarded Wife," contains the lines: "Who says that *t'u* is bitter? It is sweet as the *tsi.*"

Both examples were disputed by later historians who claimed they were fraudulent or of doubtful origin. It was proven that the *Pen ts'ao* was written first during the Later Han dynasty, two thousand years after Shen Nung's legendary life, and the reference to *t'u* was not added until after the seventh century A.D., when the Chinese character *ch'a* came into being and specifically meant tea. It simply did not exist as part of the written language before then.

Quoting from *Shih Ching* was equally susceptible to puncture. The possibility is quite strong, according to scholars, that the book did not survive the burning but is instead the product of a later disciple of Confucius who wished to perpetuate his name. Orientalists are in accord, however, that whoever edited the book did not intend *t'u*—which appears several times in *Shih Ching*—to mean tea. And in the passage cited, *t'u* translates into *sow-thistle*. It is the sow-thistle, which is sweet as the *tsi*, or *shepherd's purse*.

Why the confusion? The two-fold problem lies in interpreting *t'u*, which originally alluded to the sow-thistle, a prickly leaf plant with yellow flowers. But in the written Chinese language, ideograms are used to convey ideas, not only words. And because there is not a uniform pronunciation for each character, the characters can vary in both meaning and sound from one part of the land to another. Thus the character pronounced *t'u* came to symbolize several plants: sow-thistle, smart weed, bitter herb, flowering rush and tea.

Before the adoption of the character *ch'a* during the Later Han era, more than one symbol applied to tea: those for *chia, ming, shê, hsuan* (or *chu'an*), *yu* and *t'u*. Of them all, *t'u* seems to have been used the most for tea. When *ch'a* was created, its character was derived from that of *t'u*— a single horizontal line sets them apart—and its pronounced name approximated that for *chia*.

Once tea moved from the realm of medicinal value to that of a highly popular drink enjoyed by the masses, Oriental scholars were even more prone to interpret *t'u* as meaning tea in earlier writings, whether or not that was the intended meaning. In giving tea a longer lineage by exploiting *t'u*, they too clouded the beginnings of tea as a drink. Was it even known as a drink, albeit a bitter one, during the time of Confucius? There is not a final answer.

TEA'S FIRST PUBLISHED MENTION

The age-old enigma surrounding tea's beginnings has also covered its first credible mention in print. Much has been made of the suspect writings of Confucius, but an equal charge of fraudulent authorship was never levied against the works of his contemporary, the philosopher Yen Ying, who died in 493 B.C. If his writings were among those saved from the literary inferno of Shih-Hwang-ti, tea may well have been known as a drink during their lifetimes. Then again, the translation of the crucial character *ming* may have been one of wishful interpretation. The lines are from *Yen Tsu Ch'un Ch'iu* (the sayings of Yen Ying): "When Yen Ying was the chief official of the Duke of Ch'i, he ate unpolished rice, three roasted birds, five eggs and took *ming* and goosefoot." A heady meal, but was it capped by tea and goosefoot? *Ming* too held other meanings.

A step closer to first credible published mention lies in the written opinion of Hua T'o, a physician of considerable importance whose life spanned the first two centuries of the Christian era (he died in A.D. 220). He wrote of tea: "To drink *k'u t'u* (bitter tea) constantly makes one think better."

Less than a hundred years later, one of the Chin dynasty's top generals apparently felt that tea would make him feel young again. In a letter to his nephew Liu Yen, the governor of Yen Chou, Liu Kun wrote: "A catty of dried ginger of An Chou, a catty of the yellow-colored medicinal root and a catty of cinnamon, which I have received, are the necessary things to me. Now I feel aged and depressed and want some real tea. Send them on."

Extracts from other writings of the early Christian era skirt the credibility gap, but Orientalists have given the nod to the *Erh Ya*, a dictionary of ancient Chinese origin, for the first credible published mention. Annotated by the Chinese scholar Kuo P'o around A.D. 350, the dictionary (said to have been compiled originally by the Duke of Chou in the eighteenth century B.C.), defines tea as a beverage made from leaves by boiling, and describes the tea plant as "small like the gardenia, sending forth its leaves even in winter. What is plucked early is called *t'u* and what is plucked later is called *ming*," which, it said, was known by the people in Szechwan as bitter tea.

As described in a later dictionary—the *Kuang Ya*, published during the Later Wei dynasty (A.D. 386–535)—tea developed a spicier taste with the addition of onions, cinnamon and orange after the boiling water was poured. No wonder the dictionary also noted that the drink "renders one sober from intoxication and keeps one awake."

CULTIVATION AND TRADE COMMENCE

According to documents on file in China, the tea bush—or tree—is indigenous to the province of Hunan in southwest China, where it grew wild among the mountains and hills, thriving where the soil was particularly rocky and growing where no other plant could. Cultivation of the bush, however, began along the Yangtze River area in Szechwan Province, where it was introduced from Yunnan. The year established is approximately A.D. 350. Curiously, leaves from a bush rooted in Yunnan soil change from robust, thick and glossy specimens to thin, small, dull ones when the bush is transplanted to alien soil (be it in another province or beyond). But once back in Yunnan's earth, new growth reverts to the hardy, shiny variety.

Cultivating the
tea. Gouache in
form of wallpaper.
*Museum of the
American China
Trade, Milton,
Massachusetts.*

The tea bush is an evergreen plant related to the Camellia family. When
it was believed that two distinct tea plants existed—one in China, the other
in India—botanists gave them the formal names of *Thea sinensis*, or China
Tea and *Thea assamica*, or Assam Tea. But when it was decided that tea
was introduced to Yunnan from Assam centuries before cultivation began,
a new name was given to the single tea plant of the genus Camellia. Its
name, *Camellia sinensis*.

Singly or in a row, the tea bush is lovely to behold. Its leathery green leaves with serrated edge and sharp, tapered point are a handsome contrast to the delicate, pure-white petals of the flower that rim a profusion of yellow stamens. If left uncut, the bush becomes a tree, as nature intended, reaching perhaps forty, sixty, even seventy feet high. But the bushes are pruned constantly to allow the main stem to burst forth with new branches and are cut back to three or four feet in height and width so that pluckers can reach every leaf.

Early myths, once again placed at the door of imaginative Buddhists, say

Drying the tea.
Gouache in form
of wallpaper.
*Museum of the
American China
Trade, Milton,
Massachusetts.*

that monkeys were used initially to pluck the leaves and the buds from trees too tall to reach. Some monkeys were allegedly trained for the task while others were goaded into it. According to the improbable tale, the Chinese would hurl stones at the monkeys whom they found playing around the trees. Furious, the monkeys would break off branches from trees and shower them upon the Chinese. Fortunately, for both primates and humans, it was not a practice pursued—if ever it did exist beyond a fertile Buddhist mind.

When farmers first began plucking the leaves, they thought nothing of cutting down the trees to reach the upper leaves. But they soon realized that wanton destruction of the forest could lessen future supply and, with demand for tea growing daily, care had to be taken to meet it. Taking knowledge gleaned from other agricultural endeavors, they began improving the tea plant's development. The seeds were found to grow best in aerated soil and, for best drainage results, on the sides of mountains and hills.

It is a mark of insincerity of purpose to spend one's time in looking for the sacred Emperor in the low-class tea-shops.

ERNEST BRAMAH (E. B. Smith) (1868–1942)
The Wallet of Kai Lung, "Translation of Ling"

Cultivation spread from Szechwan through southwestern China and into the central part of the country. By the fifth century A.D., tea had joined noodles, cabbage and vinegar as a respectable article of trade. A century later it was considered more pleasurable to drink—the manufacturing qualities had improved—and special plants, those grown in Hunan and Hupeh, were cultivated solely for the emperor's teas. With the entire country tea mad, it follows that advantage of the popularity should be taken by the government. Tea was taxed in A.D. 780, the same year that saw publication of the first book on tea, but public outcry was so vocal that the tax was rescinded for thirteen years.

THE FIRST TEA BOOK

Merchants of the eighth century were no less aware of the impact a healthy publicity campaign could have on sales than are the media-conscious entrepreneurs of the twentieth century. Until publication of *Ch'a Ching,* or *The Classic of Tea,* there had not been any informative writings either on the cultivation or the manufacture of tea. What was known had been passed on virtually from one person to another. Publication of *Ch'a Ching* produced far more results than anyone anticipated. Not only did it revolutionize

China's tea industry, it served eventually as the basis for the highly complex and formal Japanese ceremonial of tea.

In commissioning Lu Yu to write *Ch'a Ching*, the tea merchants could not have bettered their choice. Here was a man whose joyous love of life and his respect for every part of it—from the smallest living thing to every viewable object and personal act—was symbolic of the attitude prevalent during the T'ang dynasty in which he lived. The T'ang era was one of territorial and cultural expansion. It saw the Chinese Empire spread out to parts of Manchuria, Tibet, Mongolia, Korea and Turkistan until finally stopped by the Arabs in West Turkistan. It saw warlords adopting various provinces for their own rule and development under the emperor and Chinese civil service examinations put into practice after careful study of Confucius's writings. In literature, poetry reached its greatest heights, and sculpture, so evident in the famous T'ang horse, attained its zenith. It was a growing period in every direction.

The essence of Lu Yu's celebration of life flows through every page of his three-volume work. But had one said to him in his younger days that one day he would author a great work, laughter might have been the response from him and those who knew him. Lu Yu was a clown, a performing buffoon who traveled throughout the provinces bringing laughter with him and leaving it behind—hardly the life expected for him by the Buddhist priest who adopted the orphan he found wandering around Fu-Chow (in Hupeh Province). The priest had thought Lu Yu would follow in his steps.

But the steps that Lu Yu longed to take were those that would lead him to the world of books. He craved to be educated, to learn about everything that had been written. Clowning brought him happy moments but nothing compared in intensity to the soaring exuberance that came when a patron of his performances became the benefactor of his education. Once Lu Yu had immersed himself in books, he wanted to write one too. The wish became reality through the tea merchants.

---

*Stands the Church clock at ten to three?
And is there honey still for tea?*

RUPERT BROOKE (1887–1915), "The Old Vicarage, Grantchester"

Endemic to the philosophy of the T'ang era was the belief in the now, the moment. This was a time when Taoism, Buddhism and Confucianism were striving for mutual harmony and synthesis in a universe that considered each minute of life as important as the hour or the day or the life. In effect it honored the particular within the universal. In harmony and order there is beauty and in beauty there is harmony and order. The governing T'ang principle of harmony and order formed the concept of *Ch'a Ching*.

Examining the tea
leaves before pick-
ing. Gouache, one
of set of four.
C. 1800–1840.
*Samuel L. Lowe,
Jr., Antiques,
Boston.*

Lu Yu's three-volume work is divided into ten parts, none less important
than another. The first part is devoted to the characteristics and cultivation
of tea. To him wild tea is superior to the garden grown; russet leaves
superior to green; tea made from new shoots superior to that made from
only the bud; tightly curled leaves preferable to the open ones; leaves
picked from a sunless area of no value at all. He emphasized that leaves
should not be picked until a plant's third year and never out of season.
Neither should they be mixed with other herbs and plants.

Part II tells of the tools used to hold the leaves while being picked, to
dry them, mash them into pieces and reroast them. The baskets should be
of bamboo; the furnace without a chimney; the boiler of wood or earthenware, and the pestle best if it has been long in use.

In Part III he writes that tea should generally be plucked during March,
April and May (although he didn't say it, the leaves can also be picked
much later). And they should never be picked when there has been rain
or there are clouds in the sky. Sun must prevail. Lu Yu wrote of tea's many
shapes, likening the leaves to creases in a Mongol's boots; the dewlap of
a wild ox, some of them sharp, others curled. Some leaves resembled a
mushroom in flight, similar to a cloud coming from behind a mountain;
others took the shape of ripples on the water. The teas from these he
deemed the finest; while those from leaves that resembled the bamboo
husk, too hard and too firm; and those from leaves that took the shape of
a sieve were old and worthless.

He numbered seven steps from picking the leaf to sealing it: in between,
steam, pound, shape, dry and tie it. He listed eight possible shapes in all,

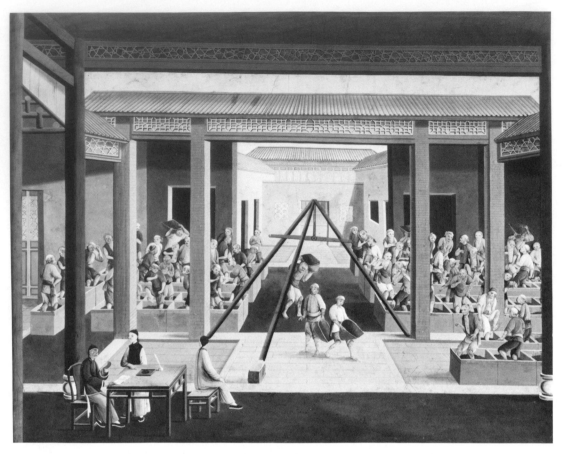

Tea processing.
Gouache. *Museum
of the American
China Trade, Mil-
ton, Massachusetts.*

and wrote that the best connoisseur of tea is not one who notes its smooth-
ness and dark liquor (the least informed) or who judges it by its yellowness
and wrinkled look (lesser informed); but one who is able to judge both its
good qualities and its bad.

Volume two begins with his devotion to the tea equipage. In all, there
are twenty-four implements necessary to preparing for tea and each must
be used every time.

The stove should be of brass or iron and tripod-shaped; the bamboo
basket fourteen inches high and with six openings; the hexagonal stoker
to be of iron and the fire tongs, cylindrally shaped and fifteen inches long,
of iron or copper.

The cauldron, usually of pig iron, should be smooth inside for easy
cleaning but could have a rough exterior to absorb the flames. Though
some cauldrons were made of tile and others of stone in different areas, the
best and the longest-lasting are of silver. "When purity is the standard, it
is silver that yields the purity" (translated by Francis Ross Carpenter). The
stand should be in the shape of a cross; the pincers of green bamboo,
fourteen inches long and split at the first inch so that sap from the bamboo
will fall into the fire when the tea is being heated. For those who do not

live near the forests, Lu Yu suggests "it is perhaps better to use pincers made of purified iron or wrought copper."

The sack chosen to store the heated tea and retain its fragrance was to be of thick white paper made from rattan; the grinder or roller of wood, the inner part rounded, the outer square, accompanied by a brush whose tip is from the feathers of a bird.

The sieve, made of bamboo and covered with gauze, is put into a casket containing a measure. The casket should be three inches high in all, with the cover taking up one inch. Lu Yu suggested that seashells, especially those of the clam or oyster, or a ladle made from bamboo, iron, or brass, serve as the measure. "To one pint of water," he wrote, "add no more than a square inch of tea." However, for those who preferred thinner tea, he suggested lowering the amount and for those enjoying heartier tea, adding more.

The water dispenser is to be made of wood and joined on the inside by lacquer; the filters of raw copper to ensure fresh water and guard against unpleasant odors. Neither iron nor wrought copper should be substituted, but for those living in the mountains or forests, wood and bamboo filters can be used. The bag that fits over the copper frame is to be made of young bamboo woven together, covered with a piece of jade-green silk, waterproofed, and then fitted with a green oiled bag for storage.

*The would-be wits and can't-be gentlemen,
I leave them to their daily "tea is ready,"
Smug coterie and literary lady.*

GEORGE GORDON BYRON, LORD BYRON (1788–1824), "Beppo"

A ladle made from a split gourd or carved wood is needed as are bamboo pincers one foot long and inlaid with silver ends. The salt container can be of stoneware, four inches in diameter if round, or shaped like a bottle or jar. The four-and-one-tenth-inch long by nine-tenths-of-an-inch wide spoon is of bamboo.

The water pot or jar can be of clay or stoneware and should hold two pints. Lu Yu termed the tea bowls from Yüeh Chou the best, followed in order of quality by those from Ting Chou, Wu Chou, Yö Chou, Shou Chou, and Hung Chou.

There must be a basket to hold cups, but no more than ten; a brush made from coconut palm strips; a scouring box with an eight-pint capacity and a container for tea dregs half its size. Two two-foot towels to clean the tea utensils; a yellow or black lacquer rack to hold all the utensils in their proper order and, to contain everything, including the rack, a bamboo carryall.

How best to brew tea opens volume three. Lu Yu warns against baking tea over a flame caught in a draft; recommends water from calm, not churning, mountain springs as the best; river water second best and well water a disaster. The water must not overboil and, when poured into cups, the tea should be frothy.

Drinking the tea covers Part VI. Lu Yu outlines the founding of tea, lists the condiments normally added to it, plus the nine steps taken to do with tea. For the best tea, no more than three cups should be taken from one tea bowl. A greater number of guests necessitates additional bowls but, he cautions: "If even one guest is missing from the assemblage, then the haunting and lasting flavor of the tea must take his place."

*We arg'ed the thing at breakfast, we arg'ed the thing at tea,
And the more we arg'ed the question, the more we didn't agree.*

WILLIAM CARLETON (1794–1869), *Farm Ballads*, "Betsey and I Are Out"

Part VII is devoted to notations on tea, from listing those who have had a role in its developments to quotations on tea from poems, books and dictionaries.

The tea-producing areas are enumerated in Part VIII, while Part IX summarizes those occasions when specific utensils need not be included in tea's preparation, but he emphasizes that if even one utensil is missing from the city home of a patrician, then tea simply cannot be served there.

With publication of Lu Yu's Code of Tea, the beverage that could delight the soul, repair inner and outer ills (it was also used as a body paste to ease rheumatic pains), stimulate the mind, and, for the Taoists, contained the needed substance to sustain immortality, was elevated to an even higher degree of eminence. And, within the home, it was the singular honor—and the duty—of the master to oversee its celebration. Neither his wife nor his servants could ever expect to preside over the tea service.

TEA CHANGES

Succeeding dynasties brought changes to tea—changes in the way that it was made, the color of the bowl from which it was poured and drunk and the philosophy that had formed its pedestal. In Lu Yu's time, tea was baked in cake form; salt was still added to the boiling water; the drink was poured into bowls and cups of glazed blue, a shade Lu Yu thought brought out the greenness in the tea; and the tea was symbolic.

During the Sung dynasty which followed the T'ang, whipped tea came into fashion. The dried leaves were ground into powder form before being whipped in hot water with the aid of a bamboo whisk and then, minus salt (cast out forever from tea), the drink was poured into heavy dark bowls.

This marked the first time that the liquid was imbibed solely for the pleasure brought by its aroma and flavor. Tea ceased to represent an ideal as it touched the senses and gave enjoyment that began to be shared by all classes. But it was not enough that the pleasures of tea be experienced only within the home. It should be taken among friends. To achieve that, tea houses sprang up in cities, giving birth to a special design of architecture, while connoisseurs enthusiastically searched for new teas. Emperor Hwei Tsung (A.D. 1101–1126) not only encouraged the cultivation of new teas, he wrote a critique on twenty different varieties, naming the "white tea" as the rarest and most delicate.

As tea evolved into a social custom among the Sungs, it became part of a ritual among the Zen Buddhist priests. Every day they gathered in front of the image of Bodhidharma and, in a solemn ceremony, sipped tea from the same bowl. Three hundred years later this ritual would develop into the stylized Japanese tea ceremony.

Here's your arsenic dear.
And your weed-killer biscuit.
I've throttled your parakeet.
I've spat in the vases.
I've put cheese in the mouseholes. Here's your
...nice tea, dear.

DYLAN THOMAS (1914–1953), *Under Milkwood*

Unfortunately, the enlightened cultural period under the Sungs came to a devastating end in the thirteenth century when Mongol tribes overran the country. For a brief period from the fifteenth to seventeenth centuries, China was reunified again under the Ming dynasty. A lightness of spirit prevailed throughout the country, which was ruled by the middle class, the feeling evidenced in the gaily colored porcelain tea services created by Ming artisans. But the Mings were not strong enough to ward off another alien invasion, and the Manchus took over.

Tea retained its place in the life of the Chinese under the Manchus but the romance surrounding it was gone forever. So were the earlier methods of preparation. Tea was neither baked nor whipped now. It was steeped in hot water before being poured into bowls. Though tea-drinking remained important within households, each one savoring its particular favorites, tea became a common staple in the home.

2

Tea in Japan

ONE DAY IN JAPAN, the Emperor Shomu summoned a hundred monks to his palace in Nara, the capital, to read from the Buddhist scriptures for four days. It was in A.D. 729, the first year of the Tempei era, and it is a date clearly marked on the tea calendar of Japan. While they were there, the emperor offered the religious some of the rare and costly *hiki-cha*, or powdered tea, that had been brought to him by emissaries to the T'ang court. The monks were so impressed with the drink that they decided the tea plant should be cultivated in Japan too, and one of the monks, Gyoki, capped his life by planting tea bushes in the gardens of each of the forty-nine temples he built.

This was during the period that Japan was struggling to emerge as a state while a sophisticated T'ang culture was flourishing in China. Because Japan lacked traditions to bolster her early endeavors, she became greatly influenced by the Chinese wealth, grandeur and accomplishments. Buddhism had come to Japan during the mid-sixth century, and Buddhists, with Japanese scholars who had ventured to China, were determined that Japan should be modeled along its lines. With the royal court's approval, missions were sent to China, where the young scholars learned all they could about the country's arts, sciences, religions, laws and forms of government. They then taught these lessons upon their return home.

Japan did not mirror China because much of the Chinese culture was adapted so that it became purely Japanese in expression. But still its effects were far-reaching, and even city planning and architecture found roots in Japan. The Japanese capital of Nara was patterned after China's capital,

Ch'ang-an, while the tea houses and gardens—especially those in Kyoto (founded A.D. 794)—followed the simple but elegant Chinese lines. Once Kyoto in the north replaced Nara as the capital, the characteristic that was to become the tea culture of Japan began to emerge from the leisurely serving of tea.

The Buddhists were greatly instrumental in tea's development. They returned from China with seeds which they planted in the temple gardens, they learned how to manufacture it and they took inventory of all the utensils required for the tea service. Ancient records confirm that tea was served in the palaces as well as in the temples. When the Imperial Palace was built in the Capital of Peace in A.D. 794, the Emperor Kammu ordered an enclosed tea garden adjacent to it and created a governmental post within the medicinal bureau to administer it.

His successor, the Emperor Saga, was so pleased with his first taste of tea at Bonshaku Temple that he ordered tea planted in the five home provinces and an annual tribute exacted for royal use. Ancient records also confirm that in every crowd there is a nay-sayer. One Buddhist priest refused to serve tea to his charges because he believed that those "who drink tea become boisterous and disorderly."

JAPAN'S FIRST TEA BOOK

Tea's popularity among the nobility and religious of Japan suffered a rude setback soon after its acceptance. In China, the T'ang dynasty was showing signs of decay and, with its weaknesses evident, Chinese influence began losing favor in Japan. The civil service and centralized form of government that had been copied was now seen as vulnerable, unable to meld well with the strong feudal philosophy extant. If a Chinese emperor could lose control, then why not a Japanese sovereign whose government was cut from the same brocade?

With the start of the tenth century it happened. Restless shoguns (feudal lords) reduced the emperor to puppet importance and the country was ruled by a series of regents. A number of them were from the Fujiwara tribe who married into the royal family to maintain control. But other shoguns wanted the power to be in their hands and the consequence was war. For nearly two hundred years Japan was infected with intermittent civil strife as shoguns tried to best each other and the warring samurai class did as the nobles bid. Tea, tea gardens and the tea service were all but forgotten.

With peace restored in A.D. 1185, Japan looked again to China for the model on which to rebuild herself. China was once more in the sun, thriving under the Sungs and communications between the two countries flowed anew. In A.D. 1191, tea was reintroduced to Japan by the man who has been called Japan's "father of tea." The Buddhist abbot Yeisei returned from China with new seeds which he planted and cultivated in three different areas. Others he gave to his colleague Myokei who sowed them in the grounds of Kosan-ji, northwest of Kyoto. The small temple garden is still there, as are offshoots of the original plantings. And tea, made from their leaves, is still served at the temple.

Had it not been for Yeisei's total commitment to tea, it is doubtful that the drink would have become such a dominant force in Japanese life and custom. The abbot, who was also head of the Zen sect of Buddhists in Japan, spread its culture and cultivation at the same time that he was promoting Rinzai Zen, imported from southern China. The two were to become synonymous.

Yeisei's belief in tea's curative powers led him to write Japan's first book on tea. *Kitcha-Yojoki* translates literally into *Book of Tea Sanitation* and, had it been authored by a copywriter on creative Madison Avenue, he might well have been asked to tone down his selling point, else no one would believe it. As it is, Yeisei is overzealous. "Tea is the most wonderful medicine for nourishing one's health . . . the secret of health lies in the well-being of the five organs. Among these five the heart is sovereign, and to build up the heart the drinking of tea is the finest method. . . .

"Our country is full of sickly looking, skinny persons and this is simply because we do not drink tea. Whenever one is in poor spirits, one should drink tea. Drink lots of tea, and one's energy and spirits will be restored to full strength."

Yeisei got the chance to prove his point when the rather obese shogun Minamoto Sanetomo (A.D. 1203–1291) overindulged himself at a meal. Convinced that he was dying, the gourmand summoned the priest to say prayers in his honor and for his recovery. Yeisei complied, but not before convincing the prostrate man to sip some liquid that he had brought with him. While the Buddhist prayed, the shogun sipped and, in short order, he was feeling well again. Miracle of miracles. Tea was given full credit for the recovery and the shogun became one of its disciples.

News of the wondrous cure fanned out, touching commoner and aristocrat alike, and immediately all began taking the drink. First it was for its supposed curative value, but soon it was for the congeniality it offered when taken within the family setting or among friends. Tea-drinking became an excuse for getting together. Eventually it also became an aesthetic rite.

TEA AND ZEN

Yeisei's preachings on Zen and on tea attracted the growing samurai class in Japan. With emphasis on learning through direct action rather than through books (words are considered an impediment), Zen's discipline appealed to the orderly military mind.

Stress is placed on self-reliance and self-discipline in order to attain the ultimate truths of Buddhism. A person does not *try* to do or to be. He does. He is. He does not try to do as his neighbor does. He is his neighbor. He does not try to be Buddha. He is the child of Buddha, therefore he is Buddha. He is the flower in the garden and the bird winging overhead. He is also the tea in the cup.

Achieving that state of nontrying, of being in direct touch with the innermost nature of things, is not, however, a plateau easily reached. Zen's lessons are passed on from master to pupil, the learning process devoted to deep meditation coupled with paradoxical conversations between tutor and student. It may take eight, ten, eleven years or longer before satori— sudden enlightenment of all things—is perceived through the freed self. It may. There is no guarantee that satori will be reached.

Following in the steps of Yeisei, other Zen priests confirmed tea's place in Zen practice and, in 1261, Eison traveled across Japan, stopping at every inn along the way, to offer tea and preach Zen to the masses who readily accepted the concept of both. Tea became a national indulgence, savored by the indigent as much as by the noble. But until the sixteenth century, Japan did not begin to develop and produce her own tea equipment. She relied on those from China, priests returning from there with their own selections for temple use while the court favored bowls from the Sung period, lacquered trays and, as caddies, medicine bottles.

CONTESTS AND CHAOS

The fourteenth century can never be described as one of Japan's better periods. Although twice during the latter part of the previous century she had repulsed the invading Mongolian forces led by the eminent Kublai Khan, the unity of spirit that characterized most of the Kamakura era (A.D. 1185–1333) fell away once peace was restored and the country entered a period of restlessness among the nobles, the samurai and the imperial court.

The tenor of the decaying spirit was reflected in the tea rooms in which gentle conviviality had been replaced by a boisterous air—a fact that the wary abbot who refused to serve tea would have appreciated, had he been around. Waves of Tea Tournaments consumed the nobles to the exclusion of more serious affairs. Contests were held based upon those for Incense Comparing, with contestants vying to distinguish *hon-cha* (real tea) from *hi-cha* (nontea or strains from other areas). There were prizes for the discerning, ranging from rich silks and brocades to paintings, jewelry, heady incense and armor. But *l'embarras de richesse* was such that the winner preferred to give away his rewards to the dancing girls and performers attendant in the tea rooms.

It was not without reason that tea-drinking began being looked upon with a negative and questioning eye. Not only were the tea rooms amok with wild behavior, as illustrations of the lolling lords proved only too clearly, but a plot against the government was found to have originated in one. In

1331, the Emperor Godaigo tried to restore imperial rule beyond the figure-head status allowed by the shoguns. But once he made that move, restlessness turned to rebellion. The noblemen withdrew to their tea rooms and games on an even grander scale, compelling the government finally to pass a law in 1336 condemning the practice of the tournaments. Notice was duly served upon the tea rooms and posted at the busier intersections. But attempts to curtail the activities were no more successful than those of the emperor to rally support. Generals defected and civil war flurried, rather than flourished, until the Ashikagas gained control in 1338.

Just how much good they accomplished can best be illustrated by noting that well into the nineteenth century, the Japanese in Kyoto could pay a few sen for the privilege of beating statues of the Ashikaga family at Toji-in. Their era, known as the Muromachi period (1338–1568) was a paradox—wars and plagues counterpointed by incredible artistic growth.

Zen power and influence was on the ascendency during this time, touching many areas. Monasteries had developed into private domains, becoming centers of art and learning while also maintaining their private armies. And priests became the confidantes of the Ashikaga shoguns, advising on trade with China, the arts and religion. The austerity and discipline of Zen was reflected in the pure, minimal brushstrokes of paintings, in the uncluttered lines and simplicity of the temples and palaces, and in the rock-and-sand temple gardens. Tea-drinking continued its wild ways for a time but in the second half of the fifteenth century, it began settling into the formalized art form under the guidance of Zen priests.

CHA-NO-YU

While noblemen had made merry in the tea rooms and power-hungry generals had joined the provincials in revolt, Buddhist priests continued with their devotion to tea and the solemn ritual of drinking it from a communal bowl before the altar of Bodhidharma.

The ceremonial drinking of tea is known by two names—*Cha-no-yu*, which translates literally into "Hot Water for Tea," and *Chado*, the Way of Tea. Those who teach it are *Cha-jin*, or Tea Men. Cha-no-yu was held in the woodland settings of the Buddhist temples, and when the Zen priests first introduced it to court and to the aristocrats of Kyoto, a separate part of the living room was screened off to serve as the tea room. Known as the *kakoi* (enclosure), it was followed by the *cha-seki*, a room set aside in the house for the tea ceremony. The altar, before which the priests stood, was represented in the home by *tokonoma*, a raised niche or alcove which held unobtrusive flowers and favored treasures of the host to honor the seasons and enlighten the guests.

Eventually, the natural setting surrounding Cha-no-yu in the temples was duplicated by creating an independent tea house apart from the private home. The *sukiya*, meaning the Abode of Vacancy or the Unsymmetrical (which the Japanese preferred over the Chinese eye for symmetry), was set in a small garden called *roji*, or "dewy path."

Roji was mandatory when a tea room was separate from the house and under Sen-no Rikyu (1521–1591), Chado's most outstanding of tea masters, *roji* was no more than a path leading from the garden gate to the tea house. Nothing was to intrude upon the guests' arrival for Chado. This insistence on lack of drama or distraction compelled Rikyu to plant a hedge at Tai-an that deliberately cut off a magnificent panorama beyond. The sand and stone and spare plantings of the *roji* were enough. They formed the quintessence of Zen's concept of *mu*, nothingness, the pure world of Buddha.

"Take some more tea," the March Hare said to Alice very earnestly. *"I've had nothing yet,"* Alice replied in an offended tone, *"so I can't take more."*

LEWIS CARROLL (CHARLES LUTWIDGE DODGSON) (1832–1898)
Alice in Wonderland, Chapter 6

Not everyone shared Rikyu's feelings for sparseness and "poverty" of expression (many tea houses cost a considerable amount to look spare and unimpressive and great pains were taken to give *roji* their casual, unimportant appearance). In later years *roji* were larger and more opulent in design while some Cha-jin took advantage of *sakkei*, or borrowed scenery, in planning their gardens.

Of the numerous Zen priests who contributed uniquely to the development of Cha-no-yu, there were three: Ikkyu (1394–1481), the prince-turned-priest who drew tea-drinking away from the nobles' boisterous ways to a closer conception of Zen; Murata Shuko (1422–1502), his pupil, who established Cha-no-yu as a definite Way of life in Japan; and Rikyu, who, among many contributions, set the rigid standards for the ceremony.

Ikkyu encouraged the young Shuko to approach the teachings of Zen by studying the Chinese version of the tea ceremony, which he did and through which he conceived Cha-no-yu into an art form. Shuko, who became one of the Zen priests advising the Ashikaga shoguns, had particular influence on the eighth shogun, Yoshimasa (1358–1408), an enigmatic man who withdrew from his responsibilities to pursue his private interests in the arts and in tea.

Living in seclusion at Ginkaku-ji palace, "Silver Pavilion," outside Kyoto, Yoshimasa spent his days indulging in his exquisite collection of tea utensils and beautifully austere Zen-inspired paintings, and in giving tea parties under the guidance of Shuko, whom he had named First High Priest of Cha-no-yu. *Matcha*—a green powdered tea whipped in boiling water as done in China—was served, and to his friends and generals, Yoshimasa rewarded loyalty and good deeds with caddies of tea rather than with armor.

(If anyone could convince Yoshimasa of the extreme importance and consequence of Cha-no-yu, it was Shuko, who, it might be said, knew both sides of the tea bowl. He once was ousted from his temple for gambling in and judging tea tournaments.)

While Shuko is said to have designed the first *cha-seki*, or separate tea room within a home (for Yoshimasa at Ginkaku-ji), Rikyu created the first *sukiya*, or separate tea house. It measured ten feet square, or, four and a half mats, was to hold no more than five guests at Chado, and included a *mizu-ya*, or anteroom, where the utensils were washed, and a *machi-ai*, or verandah, for guests awaiting the tea ceremony. The dimensions of the room in which Chado is held are determined by the number of tatami, floor mats, each of which measures three feet by six feet. The standard tea room size is four and a half mats, but a room can be as small as one and a half mats, large enough for only one person. The door of a tea room is as wide as one mat, the ceiling height one mat in length plus a few inches.

Economy of decor within the tea room—or, rather, the lack of it—was consistent with the Zen use of the monastery. It was not there to be lived in, but to sleep in. Accoutrements were not requisite to sleep. Rikyu concurred with Shuko's essence of *wabi*, a thatched hut used as a tea room. *Wabi* symbolized the contrasts and incongruities found in life and pointed out the need for harmony between both—poverty and wealth (Shuko: "It is good to see a fine horse tied to a *wabi*."); beauty in the mundane; the unexpected and the predictable (Rikyu: "Let them view a single morning-glory when they anticipate nothing."); wisdom and talent supreme in a man given but a short life.

*Twinkle, twinkle little bat
How I wonder what you're at!
Up above the world you fly,
Like a tea-tray in the sky.*

LEWIS CARROLL, *Ibid.*, Chapter 7

In absolute contrast to *wabi* was the gold-built and filled tea room that Hideyoshi, Rikyu's friend and ruler, ordered built for himself. Only the bamboo whisk, linen cloth and wooden ladle were not of gold. But then, Toyotomi Hideyoshi was himself a man of contrasts. A brilliant general and strategist, he was equally at home with scholars, poets, artists, dramatists and Cha-jins.

Hideyoshi built countless palaces, one more ostentatious outwardly than another and yet, within each, were several small, carefully designed tea rooms in which he served tea to friends. He also had a *wabi* built for him by Rikyu which he termed his favorite tea hut. It was tiny—two mats long —and very plain. No more than two could take tea there. Hideyoshi also owned a number of portable *wabi* which followed him into battle and in which he could serve tea to his generals and take tea daily in the manner Rikyu suggested in the poem: "A house is to keep out rain/Food is to prevent hunger/This is the Buddha's teaching/And the true spirit of Cha-no-yu."

It cannot be argued that Hideyoshi's influence over Chado was nearly as great as Rikyu's. Chado was essential to the general and when he became shogun, he encouraged his subjects to take up the art, augmenting the number of Cha-jin. To ensure that Chado would be the prime focus in Japan, he frowned on the pursuit of other activities that might divert both time and enthusiasm. His frown was enough. Tea soon lacked any competition.

*Why do they always put mud into coffee on board steamers?
Why does the tea generally taste of boiled boots?*

WILLIAM MAKEPEACE THACKERAY (1811–1863)
The Kickleburys on the Rhine

During his reign as shogun, Japan began developing her own tea utensils, aided by Korean ceramists brought over after one of the wars. Cha-jin started to design their own utensils which they then commissioned ceramists to carry out and Hideyoshi disbursed tea utensils as gifts and rewards for service. This gesture raised the price of and respect for tea utensils to such a degree that when his army was about to attack a castle, the enemy leader within lowered his family's collection of tea utensils, carefully wrapped in brocade, to protect them from the destruction about to ensue. Mindful of their value, Hideyoshi's soldiers gathered them up carefully at the foot of the castle wall.

The highlight, the turning point in the lives of both the shogun and the *sado*, tea master, was the historic Kitano Tea Congress. Called by Hideyoshi and planned to the last detail by Rikyu, it was to last ten days in the pine groves of Kyoto. Everyone, poor and rich alike, was invited to attend and all Cha-jin were ordered there with their tea utensils, or they had to forfeit participating in Chado forever.

Invitations were posted on all the roads and those too poor to afford tea were urged to come, nonetheless, and partake of barley instead. Nearly five hundred came and it must have presented quite a tableau—small clusters of men spread throughout the groves, myriad tea utensils on display, steam rising from countless pots of boiling water, and the sound of bubbling water a concert carried considerable distance beyond the pines.

Unfortunately, the celebration was cut short after the first full day, thanks to a general in need of Hideyoshi's help to stem a rebellion. But the spirit that pervaded the pine groves of Kyoto that day lasted well beyond its end. The Tea Meeting served as the beginning of a new era for Chado, one which brought it into every class of life and which sustained

Rikyu's thesis that reverence, purity, harmony and the abstract be its essential qualities.

Following the success of the gathering, Rikyu's name and reputation were common knowledge in Japan. He was known as the favorite of the shogun, one on whom Hideyoshi relied for advice well beyond the scope of arts. He was also *mekiki*, the supreme authority on all Japanese arts, highly paid for his job, envied by lesser Cha-jin and criticized by his contemporaries, who believed he was taking advantage of his high position. But criticism of the famous has been long known to walk in tandem with fame and none of the complaints were ever found to be justified.

RULES FOR THE TEA CEREMONY

Of Cha-no-yu, Rikyu said that it consisted of "nothing more than boiling water, making tea and drinking it." But the rules he laid down for it were not dispensed with so casually. Inherent in his choreography for the tea room is the premise that each tea ceremony is an occasion unlike the previous one. Nothing outstanding will ever occur in any of them, save the experience of touching all the senses.

Just as Cha-no-yu should never be repetitious, so must the tea room be

Tea ceremony utensils. *Japan National Tourist Organization.*

Sashitsu Sen, 15th-Generation Grand Tea Master of Urasenke School conducting a New Year's tea cere-mony, using a bowl with gold leaf inside and formal shelf "Daisu." *Tea Ceremony Society of Urasenke, Inc.*

free of repetition. Writing of the tea room in his small classic, *The Book of Tea*, Okakura Kakuzo (1862–1913) noted: "The various objects for the decoration of a room should be so selected that no color or design shall be repeated. If you have a living flower, a painting of flowers is not allowable. If you are using a round kettle, the water pitcher should be angular. A cup with a black glaze should not be associated with a tea caddy of black lacquer. In placing a vase or an incense burner on the *tokonoma*, care should be taken not to put it in the exact center, lest it divide the space into equal halves. The pillar of the *tokonoma* should be a different wood from the other pillars, in order to break any suggestion of monotony in the room." (Pages 71 and 72, Charles E. Tuttle Co., 1956.)

The tea ceremony should never include more than five guests and, while they should be known to the host, they need not be known to each other, only that they be compatible in this intimate setting. Invitations must be sent out no later than three days before Cha-no-yu is to be held.

Preparing for the ceremony is every bit as important as the procedures once it begins. The day before, the host must clean completely the tea room and sweep and water the garden. The morning of the ceremony he must clean, sweep and water again. (The sign of a dampened gate indicates that the host is ready for his guests as does the slightly opened gate.)

He then orders the menu to be served; fills the water basin with fresh water; chooses the tea utensils to be used and washes them in the prepara-tion room where he lays them in order of use; fills the tea caddy and the bowls for sweets; rakes the ashes in a prescribed fashion before placing three hand-cut pieces of charcoal upon them; hangs a scroll in the *tokonoma* (alcove) where he also arranges some flowers and prepares the incense.

When guests arrive they wait in the Arbor, where they look at the outdoor scroll that has been hung (different from the one inside) and at other objects that may have been placed there. At each Cha-no-yu there is a special guest and if he has not been indicated on the invitation, then the guests choose him from among themselves in the Waiting Arbor. If there is a very special guest invited, the host will walk out into the garden to greet him. Otherwise he remains inside until his guests have assembled and the special guest, who becomes the spokesman for the rest, so advises the host.

The host leads the way to the tea room but, before going in, each guest washes his hands and face at the water basin. Then, in single file, each enters the tea room through a low door which necessitates a crouch position and also encourages humility. For a moment the guests admire the scroll and flower arrangement and the kettle on the hearth (each of these steps is important) before sitting down in a row after the special guest is seated

Tea ceremony.
*Japan National
Tourist
Organization.*

on the tatami. The last guest to enter closes the door in such a manner that the host will know everyone is within—"in such a manner" means that the sound of the closing door must be neither too loud nor too soft, to be heard by the host but not by the guests.

Once he knows the guests are seated, the host comes in and bows. He then returns to the preparation room to bring back the charcoal scuttle and utensils needed to restart the fire. He then brings in the bowl, caddy, whisk and ladle which he cleans once again, this time before his guests. This gesture tells the guests that he is concerned with their well-being and expresses a willingness on his part to make certain that they will be served, plus that he will do the serving. The special guest then compliments the host on the scroll and its message, which has something to do with their congregation. The host also brings in the meal which may be served with the tea.

The host places two or three scoopsful of tea into a bowl, adds hot water and whisks the tea into a frothy state. He then presents the special guest with the first bowl of tea. As each succeeding guest drinks his bowl of tea, the host cleans the bowl just used by the previously served guest. After everyone has had tea, the utensils are arranged so that they can be admired and discussed by the guests. (Discussion might include the origin, color, shape or texture of the utensil.) Then, one by one, the host removes the utensils from the room, carrying them in one hand and supporting them with the other. That completed, he stands at the entrance and bows, signaling the end of Cha-no-yu.

If a meal is to be served it usually follows Cha-no-yu. In this case, the host returns to the room after removing the tea utensils and announces that he will now offer *kaiseki*, a light meal. *Kaiseki* is the name that was given to the warming stone that Zen monks used to put on their chests in cold weather. Later the name came to symbolize something that cut hunger pangs and was adopted by the tea masters.

Following a prescribed order, as with Cha-no-yu, the host brings in the food. (Rikyu considered one soup and two vegetables enough, plus some light cakes, but the meal has been enlarged since his time.) The guests are not required to eat everything placed before them, but the rules for the guests at *kaiseki*—choreographed as it is—suggest that if a guest does not like the food or thinks he will not like it, then he should leave it on the plate. In that way, it can be eaten by someone else afterward. If the guest eats some of the food on the dish, however, he should eat all of it to make less work for the host who must otherwise remove the half-touched food from the plate before washing it. Economy of movement is in consideration at all times.

Teaism, the name given by Okakura Kakuzo to the religion of aestheticism, is a discipline of the mind, the heart, the body and the spirit. Its rules may seem rigid, even dictatorial, but it is wise to remember that Cha-no-yu originated within the temples of the Zen Buddhists and reflected the life therein. Each novitiate was guided by exacting rules of movement and Cha-no-yu's code is really but an extension, a reflection of the movement of life in the temple.

Traveler's tea bowl (*cha-wan*) and accessories. Eighteenth century. *Japanese Metropolitan Museum of Art. Gift of Howard Mansfield, 1936.*

For the Japanese, Okakura wrote that it "became more than an idealization of the form of drinking; it is a religion of the art of life. The beverage grew to be an excuse for the worship of purity and refinement, a sacred function at which the host and guest joined to produce for that occasion the utmost beatitude of the mundane. The tea room was an oasis in the dreary waste of existence where weary travelers could meet to drink from the common spring of art appreciation. The ceremony was an improvised drama whose plot was woven about the tea, the flowers and the paintings. Not a color to disturb the tone of the room, not a sound to mar the rhythm of things, not a gesture to obtrude on the harmony, not a word to break the unity of the surroundings, all movements to be performed simply and naturally—such were the aims of the tea ceremony."

AFTER RIKYU

Unfortunately, the tea master fell into disfavor with his ruler. No one is completely certain why Rikyu was handed his death sentence. One theory was that he argued frequently with the shogun, his enemies took advantage of one rift and convinced Hideyoshi that the tea master would poison him at their next meeting via a potion dropped in the tea bowl. Another story says that Hideyoshi bumped into a beautiful young woman on the street, fell in love with her and wanted to marry her. The lady in question happened to be the widowed daughter of Rikyu and her father rejected the marriage offer, saying she was just getting over her husband's death and was not ready to marry anyone—including the shogun. Suffice it to say, the reason did not revolve around a tepid cup of tea served the shogun by the tea master.

The privilege—if it can be called that—of dying by one's own hand was given Rikyu, who elected to immolate himself against his sword after serving his last tea. At the end, after his guests had drunk the tea and examined Rikyu's tea utensils, he offered each of his disciples one of the utensils as a gift. Only the bowl did he keep. After looking at it once more he said: "Never again shall this cup, polluted by the lips of misfortune, be used by man." Then he broke it. With that, his guests left—save for his closest pupil—and Rikyu took off his tea gown. Underneath was his white death robe. Very slowly he examined his sword, quietly recited lines from some of his poetry, and then plunged the blade into his stomach.

His favorite pupil was his successor, but Furuta Oribe's influence—which was considerable, until he too was forced to commit ritual suicide—was not in the same vein as Rikyu's. Oribe favored a more showy approach to tea and this partiality revealed itself most in tea utensils and architecture. Both were extremely stylized.

*Tea, although an Oriental
Is a gentleman at least;
Cocoa is a cad and coward,
Cocoa is a vulgar beast.*

GILBERT KEITH CHESTERTON (1874–1936)
"The Song of Right and Wrong"

Under the Tokugawa shoguns who followed Hideyoshi, the liberal thinking of Rikyu and his ruler gave way to strict adherence to government laws. The ideal of a classless society partaking of tea was revoked. Tea was a privilege for nobility. For a time, farmers were not even allowed to drink it. Extravagance of display had crept into the ceremony with the wealth being accumulated by the merchants. Fancier utensils were created, bigger—and gaudier—tea houses built. Tea masters were not picked for their ability but for their noble blood lines. Buddhist tea declined, Confucian tea rose.

Following Rikyu's death, his family was stripped of its fortune and possessions, but after a while Hideyoshi restored everything to them. Three of Rikyu's grandsons, the sons of Sen-no-Sotan, founded three separate schools of tea—Mushanokojisenke, Urasenke and Omotesenke. Each school follows the traditions of Rikyu, the choreography only slightly different. Urasenke has branches not only throughout Japan but in cities around the world.

3

Tea Comes to
Europe

WHO INTRODUCED TEA to the Western world? A thoughtful answer might produce the name Marco Polo. After all, he traveled extensively through the Far East while serving as emissary for the man who had become his friend and admirer. In fact, he even governed the Chinese city of Yangchow for three years in the name of his mentor, Kublai Khan—plenty of time in which to absorb the customs and traditions of that land. And in his writings on his travels through China, southeast Asia and India, he recounted the wonders and splendors he had found in the Far East and wrote about things that were practically unknown in Venice and the rest of Europe. He mentioned currency made out of paper, he wrote about coal and asbestos and he described a recipe for a food dish savored by the Chinese for centuries (the forerunner of Italian ice and ice cream). But not once did he ever mention tea. Why not? Probably because the custom of drinking tea was a favorite of the people whom the Khan had conquered. Why write about the life-style of a defeated, subjugated people? It was not worthy of mention. It was not a part of his life.

Credit goes instead to another Venetian, Giambattista Ramusio, editor, compiler of works on travel, a diplomatic representative for the Venetian state, who eventually became Secretary to the Council of Ten. He is, however, best known in history for his heroic three-volume work, *Navigatione et Viaggi*, whose pages include the travels of Magellan, Marco Polo and a Persian merchant named Hajji Mahomet, who also had been to China. For some curious reason, the volumes were not published in numerical sequence, thus Number I appeared in 1550, Number III followed six years later and

Number II, containing Mahomet's narrative with an introduction by Ramusio, was printed in 1559.

Ramusio had had a long visit with the Persian on the latter's trip to Venice and, during their time together, Ramusio learned about tea for the first time. Mahomet described the plant and its growth, how the drink was made and enumerated the many medicinal values attributed to it by the people of Cathay. Ramusio's introduction reads in part: ". . . He told me that all over Cathay use was made of another plant or rather of its leaves. This is called by those people *chai catai*. . . . is commonly used and much esteemed over all these countries." According to Mahomet, no one in Cathay ever traveled without tea and would happily exchange a sack of rhubarb for an ounce of tea, and they were quite certain that if the people of Persia "and the country of the Franks" and other parts of the world ever learned about tea, their merchants would foresake buying rhubarb forever in favor of tea.

Hot on the heels of Ramusio's "tea first" was the Portuguese Jesuit Father Gaspar da Cruz who published Portugal's first (and Europe's second) mention of tea. The year was 1560, four years after the missionary landed in China to preach the Catholic doctrine in the faraway land. As translated and published in English in Samuel Purchas's travel book, *Purchas His Pilgrimes* (1625), da Cruz noted that "Whatsoever person or persons comes to any man's house of quality, he hath a custome to offer him. . . . a kind of drinke called *chia*, which is somewhat bitter, red, and medicinall, which they are wont to make with a certayne concoction of herbes."

> *But who hath seen the Grocer*
> *Treat housemaids to his teas*
> *Or crack a bottle of fish-sauce*
> *Or stand a man to cheese?*
>
> GILBERT KEITH CHESTERTON, "Song Against Grocers"

The Italian editor, the Persian merchant, and the Portuguese Jesuit lived during a period of commercial transition and expansion in Europe. It had all been made possible with Fernando Magellan's discovery in 1497 of the sea route around the Cape of Good Hope which opened a less expensive and more direct route to trade with the Far East. Until then, Venice had been the major commercial center for Western goods destined for Asia and the Orient. Articles of trade were transported from there along the overland route, a trip that was expensive, arduous and slow and always subject to the marauding whims of Arabs who controlled most of the way.

Once the Portuguese navigator returned home with news of his find, Portuguese ships lost little time in pushing for India, where they established contact before pressing on to the Orient. Their ships were the first from the Western world to reach China and to begin trading by sea. At first

China was highly suspicious of the true intent behind the newcomers' arrival, but when a diplomat was dispatched to China from the Portuguese court to explain his country's desire only to trade (as opposed to overrunning the country as had the Tartars), the Chinese emperor relented. The Portuguese could establish a commercial post on Chinese land—but Oriental prudence kept the Portuguese from setting foot on the mainland. The traders were limited to the rocky peninsula of Macao which was joined to the island of T'ang-chia-suan by a seven-hundred-foot-wide sandy isthmus on the western side of an inlet to the Canton River. No matter. By the middle of the century they were also in business with Japan and, until 1596, had an exclusive on the Oriental sea trade.

---

*Tea! thou soft, sober, sage and venerable liquid;—
thou female tongue-running, smile-smoothing,
heart-opening, wink-tippling cordial, to whose
glorious insipidity I owe the happiest moment of my
life, let me fall prostrate.*

COLLEY CIBBER (1671–1757), *The Lady's Last Stake*, Act 1, Scene 1

If the traders could not come to the mainland, the missionaries could and did—from Portugal, from France and from Italy. But nearly thirty years passed between Italy's first published reference to tea and its second. In 1588, the Florence-based author Giovanni Maffei published both *Four Books of Selected Letters from India* and the more quoted *Historica Indica*. The former contained a letter written in 1565 by Father Almeida in which he spoke of the Oriental tea custom while the latter referred to the Japanese and *chia*: "The beverage of the Japanese is a juice extracted from an herb called *chia*, which they boil to drink and which is extremely wholesome. It protects them from pituitary troubles, heaviness in the head, and ailments of the eyes; it makes them live long years almost without langor."

The following year a Venetian priest and author, Giovanni Botero, published *On the Causes of Greatness in Cities* in which he said: "The Chinese have an herb from which they press a delicate juice which serves them instead of wine. It also preserves the health and frees them from all those evils that the immoderate use of wine doth breed in us." Again and again, tea's worth as a medicine and veritable cure-all appeared whenever written about in the Western world. Did these early missionaries to the Orient really have proof of its touted potential? It would seem so.

In 1610, a French Jesuit published the papers of the Italian priest and diplomat, Matteo Ricci, who, after waiting two years to be received at the royal court in Peiping, became one of its scientific advisers and remained there until he died nine years later in 1610. His tea narrative not only informed the reader of *cia*'s price, he also compared the Japanese method of preparing tea with that in China:

I cannot pass by some rarities as their shrub whence they make their *Cia*. They gather the leaves in the shadow, and keep it for daily dedoction, using it at meals, and as often as any guest comes to their house; yea, twice or thrice if he make any tarrying. This be beverage is always drunk or rather sipped hot, and on account of a peculiar mild bitterness is not disagreeable to the taste; but on the contrary is positively wholesome for many ailments if used often. And there is not alone a single quality of excellence in the leaf, for one surpasses the other, and thus you will often buy some at one gold escu or even two or three escus a pound, if it is rated as the best. The most excellent is sold at ten and more, often at twelve gold escus a pound in Japan, where its use is also somewhat different from that of China. For the Japanese do mix the leaves reduced to a powder, in a cup of boiling water to the amount of two or three tablespoonsful and swallow this potion mixed in this manner. But the Chinese toss a few leaves into a pot of boiling water; then, when it is touched with the strength and virtue of the same, they drink it quite hot and leave the leaves.

If tea was offered two or three times to the same person on one visit in the houses of Peiping, it was another matter with another meaning elsewhere. According to the London edition (1655) of Father Alvaro Semedo's *The History of the Great and Renowned Monarchy of China*: "In some provinces, the often presenting of this drink (*cia*) is esteemed the greater honor. But in the province of Hamcheu, if it be brought for the third time, it intimateth to the visitant that it is time for him to take his leave." On the other hand, "If the visitant be a friend, and maketh any stay, presently there is a table set with sweetmeats and fruit; nor do they ever make drie visits; which is the custom almost of all Asia, contrary to the use of Europe."

While Portugal was reveling in her exclusive dealings in the Far East, Dutch ships usually picked up the goods brought back to Lisbon (silk, china, jewelry and other riches) for transport to other European ports. But after the Dutch navigator Jan Hugo van Linschooten published his account of life while aboard a Portuguese ship in the Orient, the Dutch became thoroughly intrigued with the East and wanted direct trade also. They got their chance.

Free yourself from the slavery of tea and coffee and other slopkettles.
WILLIAM COBBETT (1762–1835), *Advice to Young Men,* Letter 1

The same year that van Linschooten's book was published—1596—the Portuguese, perhaps foolishly but for reasons of war, closed her harbors to Dutch ships. As part of the Low Countries, the Netherlands had been embroiled in struggles to free itself from the harsh and unwelcome rule imposed upon it in 1555 when Charles V, the Holy Roman Emperor, so kindly gifted the land to his son and heir, Philip II of Spain. This meant that Flanders, where he had grown up, Zeeland, Gelderland and the Netherlands were now his domain. Immediately Philip enlisted the aid of the Duke of Alba to bring the notorious Spanish Inquisition into play in a land that had known considerable commercial success and certain provincial independence and reduce it to a mere Spanish province.

For a brief period the Duke succeeded, but under the agile leadership of William the Silent, Prince of Orange, the northern provinces—which included the Netherlands—shook off the Spanish intrusion in 1574; the southern ones did the same two years later. Unfortunately for them, Spanish rule returned to the south in 1578 and further attempts to be rid of it were not entirely successful until 1609.

*They are at the end of the gallery;
Retired to their tea and scandal, according to their ancient custom.*

WILLIAM CONGREVE, (1670–1729)
The Double Dealer, Epistle Dedicatory, Act 1, Scene 1

When access to the coveted Oriental goods was cut off by the petty Portuguese, the Dutch took the only steps they could. They made plans to sail their own ships to the Far East, arriving in Java a year later. The first four ships to sail returned with a bounty of rich cargoes and the friendship of the island's natives, who were quite willing to trade. Heady with the news, Dutch merchants dispatched more ships, the numbers increasing each year until, in 1602, nearly seventy ships made the voyage.

Bad was to follow good. The veritable milking of the Indies trade flooded the market at home, sank prices to the bottom and drowned many a greedy merchant. Those who managed to survive with their wits intact wisely decided to unite in 1602 under charter of the Dutch East India Company. (The English had formed a similar company two years earlier.) The Company was headed by the Lords Seventeen, a board whose members comprised the leading merchants from each of the provinces. Control of trade was now in the hands of a single group, as was any government action undertaken in the Far East and any decisions to war with Spain and Portugal.

THE FIRST SHIPMENT OF TEA

The first recorded Dutch purchase of tea was in 1607 when a small amount was bought from the Portuguese in Macao and sent to Java. Three years later contact was made with the Japanese and tea from the island of Hirado was bought, shipped to Java and thence home. Those teas were the very first to arrive in Europe.

Afternoon tea. Etching by Pieter v.d. Berghe. C. 1700. *Museum Boymans-van Beuningen, Rotterdam.*

Having kept a low profile—compared to the Portuguese, whose missionaries were very busy trying to convert all of Japan—the Dutch were given permission to set up their own trading depot on the island. But, before long, the emperor ordered all the Europeans to quit his land. There had been one conflict too many between the Portuguese and the Japanese. While upset at the turn of events, the Dutch were willing to comply but the Portuguese were not. They lodged themselves in a high-walled settle-

Teas of the World

Tea saleswoman
in streets of Hol-
land. Painting by
Cornelis Dusast.
1700. *Museum
Boymans-van
Beuningen,
Rotterdam.*

ment above the harbor of Nagasaki, and the Japanese soldiers could not
rout them. It took the guns from Dutch ships to level their refuge. A
grateful emperor allowed the Dutch to stay but gratitude came wrapped in
restrictions. The traders were to leave Hirado for the island of Deshima in
Nagasaki Harbor and conduct their business from within a walled settle-
ment. Expanding trade with the rest of Japan was limited and the Dutch
abandoned their interests in Japanese teas to concentrate on those of China.

Their flirtation with Japan was countered by their almost total control
over the Molucca Islands spice market. To handle the flow of this lucrative
trade, the Dutch built the city of Batavia on Java, and when the English
settled on one of the Molucca Islands, the Dutch—claiming priority of settle-

ment—rebelled. The massacre of Amboyna in 1623 resulted and the
English retreated. For a number of years they would remain dependent
upon the Dutch for their supplies of tea, but the day would come when
the sun of the English would far outshine that of the Dutch or the Portuguese in the Orient.

39

*Tea
Comes to
Europe*

CHINA AND THE DUTCH

If the Dutch thought that their presence in China would be received with
a warmer welcome than that exhibited in Japan, they were quite in error.
Claiming kinship to the Ch'in dynasty (221–207 B.C.), the Manchus
overran China in 1644 and established the Ch'ing dynasty. Though fully
supported by the many tribes, the Manchus were uneasy, as if the cognate
thread might unravel at any time and the introduction of an outside influence could be the catalyst. Naturally they could not know that the Ch'ing
dynasty would last until 1912. So the Manchus continued to ignore the
periodic overtures made by the Dutch through their government at Batavia.

> *Now stir the fire, and close the shutters fast,*
> *Let fall the curtains, wheel the sofa round,*
> *And, while the bubbling and loud hissing urn*
> *Throws up a steamy column and the cups*
> *That cheer but not inebriate, wait on each,*
> *So let us welcome peaceful ev'ning in.*
>
> WILLIAM COWPER (1731–1800), "The Task"

The breakthrough came with the arrival in Batavia of a Jesuit who had
just left China after ten years. Martin Martynsen brought news that the
new emperor had decreed Canton an open port to foreign trade. How right
he was remained to be seen with the immediate dispatch of one Dutch ship
laden with goods from the island of Taiwan. Upon its return, the ship's
captain presented a letter addressed to the commander in chief at Taiwan.
The official document suggested that if the Dutch were interested in free
trade with China, an ambassador should be sent—with plenty of presents
for the emperor.

News of the summons (and the request) was passed on to the Lords
Seventeen, who decided it should be fulfilled. The initial encounter is aptly
described by Johann Nieuhoff in *An Embassy from the East India Company
of the United Provinces to the Great Tartar Cham Emperor of China*
(published in Amsterdam in 1665, in London in 1669). The Dutch were
greeted effusively by the Cantonese officials:

At the beginning of dinner, there were several bottles of *Thea* served to the table, whereof they drank to the Embassadours, biding them welcom; this drink is made of the Herb The or Cha after this manner: they infuse half a handful of the Herb The or Cha in fair water, which afterwards they boyl till a third part be consumed, to which they adde warm Milk about a fourth part, with a little Salt, and then drink it as hot as they can well endure. The Chinese boast as much of the excellency of this infusion, as the alchymists of the vertues of their expected Elixir.

More celebrations and teas—this time in Peking—and the Dutch entourage returned to Java with a letter from the emperor to the Company's governor general in Batavia. The emperor acknowledged the Dutch desire to trade with his country. He also acknowledged how profitable this could be for his countrymen. However—and it was a long however—bearing in mind that their home country (Netherlands) was far away, that travel on the high seas amid winds and storms can be perilous (with the danger extended on lengthy trips) and that if something untoward were to occur en route or on return it would dismay the emperor greatly, he had a suggestion. If they wished to trade, fine. But the traders were to show up in Canton only once every eight years with no more than a hundred men from the Company. Of that number, twenty could land and come to "the place where I kept my Court; and then you may bring your merchandizes ashore into your Lodging, without bartering them at sea before Canton."

The invitation could hardly be termed open door, but at least it could be described as ajar. Mindful of their present successes in the Indies and the possibilities of greater fortune through China trade, however limited, the Dutch agreed and China teas (plus silks and other goods) began to be imported to Europe.

PRAISE AND DISPRAISE

Tea did not tiptoe into Europe. As greater quantities arrived, paeans to its medicinal worth flowed fast and far until finally challenged in 1635. The first "tea heretic" was a German physician named Simon Pauli who believed the plant to be nothing more than the common myrtle which could be found almost anywhere in the world. As to its curative values, they were nonexistent, at least not in Europe. The point was made in his medical treatise *Commentarius de Abusu Tabaci et Herbae Thee*: ". . . it may be admitted that it does possess them in the Orient, but it loses them in our climates where it becomes on the contrary very dangerous to use. It hastens the death of those who drink it, especially if they have passed the age of forty years."

A totally opposite view was held by another doctor, this one Dutch, who consumed tea daily and died at eighty-one. But, because he was so well known in his field, Dr. Nicholas Dirx chose to express his opinion under the safety of a nom de plume. *Nikolas Tulp*'s commentary, appearing in *Observationes Medicae* in 1641, echoed the sentiments of the Orient: "Nothing is comparable to this plant. Those who use it are for that reason alone exempt from all maladies and reach an extreme old age." He then proceeded with a litany of ailments, all of which could be either cured or prevented by drinking tea, and nearly all of which can be found listed in the pages of *Ch'a Ching*.

Between 1635 and 1657, a Ping-Pong of opinions on tea ricocheted through Europe. While the highly conservative French doctor, Guy Patin, called tea "an impertinent novelty of the century," fellow colleague Philibert Morisset saw it as a "panacea." This viewpoint sent the medical world into such a frenzy that not one French doctor would stand by either Morisset or his statement. The doctor was roundly censured by a full-seated Collège de France which, at the same time, condemned tea and called for its banishment. The French, however, continued to drink it.

Tea, though ridiculed by those who are naturally coarse in their nervous sensibilities . . . will always be the favored beverage of the intellectual.

THOMAS DEQUINCEY (1875–1859)
Confession of an English Opium Eater

A German doctor thought tea could cure pernicious diseases, but a German Jesuit, Martino Martini, blamed tea for the dried-up look of the Orientals. On the other hand, the French missionary, Alexander de Rhodes, credited the Orientals' long life to tea. A Dutch doctor called it "dishwater."

In *Voyages et Missions Apostoliques*, printed in 1653, de Rhodes—who had lived thirty years in China—wrote: "I have dilated somewhat from my discourse on the subject of tea because since I have been in France, I have had the honor to see some people of great quality and of excellent merit whose life and health are extremely necessary to France, who make beneficial use of it and who have been kind enough to want me to tell them what my experience of thirty years had taught me concerning this great remedy."

One of those of "excellent merit" and "necessary to France" was the French statesman, Cardinal Mazarin, who took tea to cure his gout. When the acerbic Patin learned that, he lashed out in a letter that asked: "Isn't this a powerful remedy for the gout of a favorite?" The letter was written in the spring of 1657 but by year's end, Patin was forced to back down from his vehement stand against tea. The young son of a French surgeon, Pierre Cressy, researched the effects of tea on gout and presented his findings in a four-hour dissertation before the Faculté de Medicine. His arguments in its favor were so persuasive that the medical profession withdrew from its hostile attitude and members began to indulge too, taking tea as a drink *and* as something to smoke.

Of all the Europeans contributing to tea's popularity on the continent, there is one who outdid all the others in enthusiasm and promotion. Dr. Cornelius Decker was an eminent physician from Holland who was as well known by his nickname, "Dr. Botenko" (meaning "Dr. Good Tea"), as he was by his true name. Dr. Decker advocated tea under all conditions and in all circumstances. Between forty and fifty cups a day were to be taken to reduce a high fever, a prescription he claimed had worked for several patients, and there was no reason to limit oneself to those figures if more cups were desired. Even one hundred wouldn't be too much, he said.

"Polly, put the kettle on, we'll all have tea."

CHARLES DICKENS (1812–1870), *Barnaby Rudge*

Dr. Botenko also said tea should be taken by everyone, inside Holland and out, old and young, poor and rich, women and men. Those just becoming acquainted with tea would do well to begin by drinking only eight cups a day, gradually working up to whatever amount their stomachs would tolerate comfortably. His tea spirit was contagious. Sales soared, the company directors were ecstatic and the net result was a handsome gift of money for the doctor. Dr. Decker's reputation, however, has been slightly tarnished by the thought—nay, the probability—exercised even in his day that he was already on the company ledger as an employee.

TEA AMONG THE EUROPEANS

The German palate never really acquired the taste for tea. The controversies had left a pall on the market and preference leaned to coffee and hot chocolate. But even that brought trouble. In 1747, Frederick II of Prussia (also known as The Great) condemned chocolate as a base import and forbade its being hawked on the streets. It was left to the French and to the Dutch to experiment with tea, embrace it and adopt it as part of the daily diet. But of the two countries, its influence remained strongest in Holland, which became second to England among nations consuming the largest amount annually.

Tea was first sold from apothecary shops, a natural outlet, considering its alleged medical prowess. In Holland it moved to the shelves of stores holding spices and sugar and by the early eighteenth century, shops devoted solely to tea, or offering both coffee and tea, were open. A census taken in the city of Leiden in 1749 listed five shops selling tea only, fifty which also sold coffee, and about one hundred which offered only coffee. To distinguish the tea shops from the others, shopkeepers hung signs outside. One might illustrate a large tea bush, another would show a bush with a Chinese standing next to it, while those offering both the bean and the leaf would show two bags printed with "Coffee" and "Tea." One shop even carried a message of advice:

> Do not pass here
> when you look for good tea.
> Look, smell and taste
> as you wish
> but take some along.

By 1680, the poor of Holland were buying tea as well as the rich, and it was the custom of each household for the woman to make the selection. Once at the tea shop she would smell the different leaves packed in the bins, returning again and again to savor the essences of a few, lingering over some more than over others before being offered to chew a few leaves whose perfume she favored particularly. Once the choice was narrowed even further, a small amount of a selected tea was brewed in a little experimental pot called "Upperken" (untranslatable) or "Vinkerpootje" (one of whose meanings today is "the foot of a stove"). Two or three teas might be steeped before the final purchase was made. A number of the brewing pots were kept by the shopkeepers, but many were privately owned and brought each time by the customer.

1680 was the year in which the first mention of milk being added to tea was made in Europe. The reference appeared in one of the 1500 letters (most of them addressed to her daughter) written by the witty and acute observationalist of social history, Marie de Rabutin-Chantal, Marquise de Sevigné. Her friend, Mme. de la Sablière, had poured milk into her tea. In other letters she wrote that one friend usually drank twelve cups a day while another, on the brink of death, had been saved by consuming forty. With the introduction of coffee and chocolate as a drink, tea lost its place as a favorite in France in the closing years of the seventeenth century.

TEA-DRINKING OUTDOORS

Though in each of the homes of the wealthy a separate room was set aside for tea-drinking (with some of the poor managing to have their much smaller "tea corners"), the drink was also enjoyed outdoors. Those in a hurry or reluctant to sit inside a tea shop on a sunny day could buy a cup of tea with milk from a woman in the streets. With either a wheelbarrow or table beside her, on which rested a kettle, pitcher of milk, cups and other utensils, she would hawk her products down one street and then another. Tea was considered important enough at country fairs to be included in the banner advertising and, at the annual neighborhood gatherings at which a meal was served, tea was always on the menu.

Tea also held a prominent place in the running of Dutch inns, most of which served as stopping-off places for passengers from canal boats and stages. A complete tea service, including portable metal stove and kettle, was put at the disposal of a guest taking tea in the garden so that the thirst might be quenched easily through the passing hours.

The eighteenth century saw the development of private tea houses on the grounds of the wealthy who lived beyond the city walls. Many of these houses evolved from garden pavilions which had been built to serve as momentary shelters from sun or rain, as quiet retreats in which to receive friends or, in those gardens which ran down to the rivers or canals, as galleries from which to watch the passing boats. Originally, the houses were fairly simple in design, their roofs pyramid-shape. But with the periodic takeover of Holland by France, the French influence became evident. This influence was itself predicated on the designs of the Orient. Second-floor balconies ran around the houses whose roofs were now intricate imitations of those in the Orient. The domes were six- or eight-corner shapes, ornamental spires accenting each point, and a tier spire rising from the center. Later, new pavilions would reflect the Moorish architecture and

Hand-painted Delft blue pottery. "Lady pouring tea for those engaged in tobacco trade." 1790. *Museum of Douwe-Egberts Royal Factories, Utrecht.*

then the Gothic. Any Dutchman unable to decide on which style his tea
house should follow could choose from a wealth of designs illustrated as
a guide in magazines and books.

THE COMPANY

In Holland, the Dutch East India Company was commonly referred to as
the V.O.C. which stands for *Verenigde Oost-Indische Compagnie.* That
translates into United East India Company. While the Lords Seventeen sat
at Amsterdam, V.O.C. also had offices in five other cities: Delft, Middel-
burg, Rotterdam, Enkhuizen and Hoorn. Each of the six offices was responsible for its own ships and shipments and though the shipments were
auctioned in the respective ports instead of being transported from one to
another, all decisions—including auction dates—were made by the directors.

Before each auction took place, the V.O.C. published pamphlets detailing
the time and place of the auction, what was to be sold, a detailed description of each article and the quantity. One Company notice for November
and December 1733 announced 571,195 pounds of China tea would be
auctioned in Amsterdam while 454,054 pounds of blended teas would be
sold in the other ports.

A notice from the Lords Seventeen to the governor general at Batavia
in 1637 announced that "as tea begins to come into use with some of the
people, we expect some jars of Chinese, as well as Japanese tea with each
ship." In spite of the request, only thirty pounds of tea in all was imported
by eleven ships on their return home the end of 1650 (it took a year for
the ships to make the round trip). But thirty-five years later, the picture
had changed considerably.

The hot water is to remain upon it [the tea] *no longer than while*s *you
can say The Misere Psalm very leisurely.*

SIR KENELM DIGBY (1603–1665)
The Closet Opened, "Tea with Eggs"

In a letter dated 1685 to the governor general, the Lords Seventeen
wrote: "We have resolved to augment the demand, lately made by us, to
20,000 pounds, on condition that it be good fresh tea, and packed in such
a way as we have exposed in our demand; for as we have formerly written,
tea deteriorated by age and bad tea are naught worth any money."

By 1734, more than eight hundred thousand pounds were shipped home;
by 1739, tea outranked all other shipments from the Indies in value; by
1750, black tea superseded greens in purchase and the drink itself was

preferred to coffee by most at breakfast. By 1784, more than three million pounds a year were being imported.

It was not uncommon during the eighteenth century for samples of tea to be distributed among the potential buyers so that the tea, once bought, could remain in the warehouses until the purchaser was ready to receive it. Storage charges were included in the purchase price and the purchaser received proof of ownership from the warehouse in the form of a document carrying his name. In time these documents were traded as securities and the text was amended to justify the holder's demand for the tea.

Political controversies and wild speculations played havoc with the tea auctions during the second half of the eighteenth century. Private auctions were organized to sell the remaining teas still held by speculators and those

Tea flyer for E. Brandsma, Dutch tea merchant. 1890. *Gemeentelijke Archiefdienst Rotterdam.*

Delft teapot under
influence of
Chinese porcelain.
Late seventeenth
century. *Museum
Boymans-van
Beuningen,
Rotterdam.*

teas which had come from foreign countries. In 1791 The Hague passed
a law forbidding the sale in Holland of any teas brought in on foreign ships.

Strong competition from other East India companies cut into V.O.C.'s
foreign trade and its profits. Matters were made worse when the British
ousted the Company from its holdings in India and Ceylon. In an effort to
survive, the Company strengthened its interests in the East Indies, but at
great expense. By century's end, the V.O.C. was awash in scandal and
corruption and, nearly bankrupt, it was dissolved. Its holdings were absorbed
into the Dutch colonial empire, as was the colony it had established in
1652 at the Cape of Good Hope. That remained Dutch until overrun by
the British in 1814.

4

The English Discover Tea

IT IS HARD to conceive of a time in England—indeed, of a time throughout the British Empire—when an entire day could pass without tea ever having been served. It is far easier to envision Good Queen Bess listening to the latest reports of Essex's costly exploits in Ireland while sipping morning tea, her temper rising with each quick, deliberate raising of cup to lips. Or to imagine her father Henry VIII, the royal silver tea service and rich tea cakes before him, waiting rather impatiently for his wife to pour the first cup. It would of course be an afternoon ritual, one in which only the hand that held the teapot would change—six times, to be exact.

Tea and the tradition of afternoon tea are as closely woven into the fabric of British life as is the family royal and all its courtly doings. But there really was a time when tea was both a commodity and a drink totally unknown to every Englishman. It was never celebrated in a Richard Lovelace verse. Neither was its taste savored, admired or scorned by any of Shakespeare's characters.

Ironically, the first mention of tea in the English language occurred with the translation of a foreign work. In 1598, five years before the death of Elizabeth I, van Linschooten's travels were published in London where his comments on the Japanese drinking of *chaa* left an impression that can be termed negligible at best. Seventeen years passed before the first documented reference to tea by an Englishman was made. In a letter now in the London archives of Britain's East India Company, Richard Wickam, a Company factor stationed in Firando (Hirado), Japan, requested of Mr. Eaton, an agent at the Company's office on the island of Macao, China: "I pray you buy for me a pot of the best sort of *chaw* in Meaco."

In volume three of *Purchas His Pilgrims*, published in 1625, Samuel Purchas, clergyman and collector of literature on travel, noted: "They [referring to the Chinese] use much the powder of a certaine herbe called *chia* of which they put as much as a Walnut shell may containe into a dish of Porcelane, and drink it with hot water." He also made note that *chia* was used in "all entertainments in Iapon and China" and that it was of particular benefit to one's health. "Their alwaies drinking their drinke hot and eating little fruit (for they are not so greedie of it as our men are) doth keepe them from many infirmities and sicknesses, and therefore they live healthfully."

When it finally came time to adopt a new word into the English language, however, *chaw, chia* and other approximations of *ch'a* were passed over in favor of the name by which *ch'a* was known in the Amoy district, whose port became the main base for the English traders in 1644. *Tay* or *tchae* was anglicized into *tea*.

Early English users of tea might have enjoyed it more had they harkened either to the writings of the Dutchman van Linschooten or their own Purchas. Instead, perhaps resulting from word association coupled with unfamiliarity with the new product, some Englishmen initially chewed *chaw* and tossed out the liquid. Others chose to boil a pile of tea rather than a Walnut shell full, which they then mixed well with salt and butter before offering it to polite, probably curious, but no doubt somewhat hesitant guests.

TEA ARRIVES IN ENGLAND

Given tea's importance in the daily habits of the English, one might think there would be a marker planted somewhere on which a venerable inscription would record the very first arrival of tea on to England's shores. But no such marker exists. A rather tasty fantasy alluding to its introduction tells of a bouquet of flowers sent to one Lady Mary Douglas in London by her lover in China—presumably on duty with the Company. By the time the bouquet reached her it had faded, but Lady Mary dunked it into a vase beside her bed. In the middle of the autumn night she awoke, thirsty but unwilling to step out into the cold room for the water pitcher sitting on the chest. So she reached for the vase and, if we are to believe this, drank what might be called the first vase of tea. The bouquet had been gathered from the flowers of the tea plant but no date of its arrival accompanies the fable.

According to records of the East India Company, its first purchase of tea was a mere two pounds, two ounces worth, a gift intended for King Charles from a grateful Company (a mere pittance of thanks when measured against the Company's monopolistic earnings). Even then, the purchase of the tea was done only because the Company's request for other rarities brought over on its ships had gone unheeded. The Company directors were advised to give the king a silver case of oil of cinnamon and "some good *thea.*" The year was 1664, sixty-four years after the Company was founded, forty-nine years after Wickam wrote Eaton, seven years after tea was first sold publicly in London, and five years before tea began arriving regularly in England on Company ships. In 1666, the Company presented the king with another present—this time, nearly twenty-three pounds of "raretypes" of tea.

It is worth mentioning that the Company proffered a similar gift of tea (two pounds, two ounces) to the Russian tsar through his emissary in Delhi, who promptly refused the gift. To carry it back to Tsar Alexis, he explained, would burden him unnecessarily with a worthless commodity. Needless to say, he obviously lacked a good eye to the future. Of all the countries beyond the boundaries of the British Empire, it was Russia who took to tea with equal fervor, seriousness of purpose and commitment.

TEA AND THE COFFEE HOUSES

The first tea offered for sale to the English public came from the shelves of a coffee house in Exchange Alley. Its owner was Thomas Garway (or Garraway), also a tobacconist, who would later issue the famous tea broadside. The year of the sale was 1657.

Unknown before England's Civil War, coffee houses began springing up with fair regularity not long after coffee was introduced to England by the Greeks. The first house opened at Oxford in 1650, its popularity with students and financial success soon duplicated at Cambridge and, in 1652, the first one opened in London's Cornhill. By 1661, more than a dozen were thriving throughout the City, each offering coffee, ales and spirits, and eventually, chocolate and tea, plus free newspapers.

The progress of this famous plant has been something like the progress of truth; suspected at first, though very palatable to those who had courage to taste it; resisted as it encroached; abused as its popularity seemed to spread; and establishing its triumph at last, in cheering the whole land from the palace to the cottage, only by the slow and restless efforts of time and its own virtues.

ISAAC D'ISRAELI (1766–1848)
Tea. Curiosities of Literature

According to a London newspaper of the time, the *Mercurius Politicus Redivivus*: "There is a Turkish drink to be sold, almost in every street, called Coffee, and another kind of drink called Tee, and also a drink called Chocolate, which was a very harty drink." Coffee cost twopence, a dish of tea a ha'penny less, a drink of chocolate a ha'penny more.

Talk flowed easily in the coffee houses, the lighting of a pipe traditionally signaling that its smoker was ready to join in good talk with anyone who might be so like inclined. Politics was a favorite daily subject. The years of the Reformation were ending, Cromwell would be dead in 1658, his weak son unable to hold the country together and a new era filled with promise—the Restoration—would begin with the return of Charles II to England from exile in Holland on May 25, 1660.

In tandem with tradition, reputation eventually dictated who would visit which coffee houses. Military officers chose Little Devil Coffee-House in Goodman's Field, while clergymen preferred Child's in St. Paul's Church-yard. Lawyers and scholars frequented The Grecian at Devereux Court and Nando's, above Rainbow Tavern on Inner Temple Lane. Behind Charing Cross, Man's Coffee House catered to stockjobbers. Artists gathered at Old Slaughter's in St. Martin's Lane, authors at Button's on Bow Street. Down at the corner of Bow and Russell, in Covent Garden, Will's was crowded with men of letters and rapier-sharp wits of the day. It was at Will's that the poet Dryden held court for many years, his place of honor a chair by the fireplace in winter, on the balcony in summer.

He traces the steam engine always back to the tea kettle.

BENJAMIN DISRAELI (1804–1881)
Speech before House of Commons, 11 April 1845

Politicians and the fashionable had a choice of houses to patronize: the Cocoa Tree, Ozinda's in Pall Mall and, among those in St. James, White's. By century's end, coffee houses neared the five hundred mark in London alone, a few of less reputable fame serving as a loose covering for brothels. A number of the houses welcomed a homogenous patronage but others were distinctly elite, forerunners of the exclusive men's clubs that became such a dominant element in the life of an English gentleman, many of which survive today. One coffee house, owned by Edward Lloyd and called Lloyd's, was visited by shipowners, merchants and marine insurers. From its humble beginnings it developed into the worldwide insurance firm whose main business is underwriting marine insurance.

Coffee houses and their influence declined during the nineteenth century almost in direct proportion to the number of private clubs that opened. But, at one point during the latter part of the 1600s, the English government, vexed by their power, considered them a danger not to be ignored. The effectiveness of the proclamation demanding that the houses be closed (all licenses to be revoked) can best be shown chronologically.

The royal decree was drawn up December 23, 1675, signed by Charles II, issued December 29, 1675, and revoked January 8, 1676. Historians would be hard put to find many royal proclamations issued and reclaimed with such swiftness. To save royal face, the new proclamation voiding the first one stated that the king, in his compassionate wisdom and consideration, would allow the houses to remain open until the end of June. Neither he nor his government had anticipated the unified wrath (and strength thereto) of all who frequented the houses, their owners, and the merchants of tea, coffee, chocolate and tobacco. June 24, the new deadline, passed without incident. Nothing more was ever heard on the subject.

THE FAMOUS TEA BROADSIDE

Safely ensconced in the British Museum of London is Thomas Garway's broadside or shop-bill which he published from his coffee house in 1660. Entitled "An Exact Description of the Growth, Quality and Vertues of the Leaf TEA," the sheet tells of tea's first use "as a regalia in high treatments and entertainments, and presents made thereof to princes and grandees." Tea, he wrote, then cost between six to ten per pound (comparable to between thirty and fifty dollars a pound in the old days when the dollar was secure).

According to Garway's broadside—and in the manner in which it was written:

> The Leaf is of such known vertues, that those very Nations famous for Antiquity, Knowledge, and Wisdom, do frequently sell it among themselves for twice its weight in silver, and the high estimation of the Drink made therewith had occasioned an inquiry into the nature thereof amongst the most intelligent persons of all Nations that have travelled in those parts, who after exact Tryal and Experience by all ways imagineable, have commended it to the use of their several Countries, for its Vertues and Operations, particularly as followeth, viz: The Quality is moderately hot, proper for Winter or Summer. The Drink is declared to be most wholesome, preserving in perfect health until extreme Old Age.

*Teas,
Where small talk dies in agonies.*

PERCY BYSSHE SHELLEY (1792–1822)
Peter Bell the Third, Part III, Stanza 12

The "vertues" attributed to tea then followed, fourteen in all. In short, tea made the body "active and lusty," cured headaches and giddiness; cleansed the spleen and flushed away stones and gravel (especially when drunk with "Virgins Honey instead of Sugar"); helped breathing, cleared one's vision; wiped away laziness and purified "hot Liver"; strengthened the stomach muscles, thus aiding both a good appetite and digestion (espe-

cially effective for the more corpulent "and such as are great eaters of
Flesh").

The drink prevented dream-filled nights, eased the Brain and boosted
Memory; cut down the need for sleep; cured agues and fevers; did wonders
for the intestines (when prepared with Milk and Water); prevented consumption and constipation; cured colds, dropsies and scurveys when properly administered (meaning, hot enough to cause sweat); and rid collick
produced by gas.

Garway's phenomenal claims closed with the comment,

> And that the Vertues and excellencies of this Leaf and Drink are many
> and great is evident and manifest by the high esteem and use of it (espe-
> cially of late years) among the Physitians and knowing men in France,
> Italy, Holland and other parts of Christendom.

The miracles of tea were no less wondrous in England (if Garway were
to be believed) than they were in China. On October 20, 1686, Thomas
Povey, Member of Parliament, translated the Chinese praise of tea which
cited twenty particular virtues. Many were found in the broadside too.
Among those that weren't: "[tea] consumes Rawnesse. . . . makes one
Nimble and Valient. . . . Drives away feare. . . . Strengthens the use of
due benevolence."

PEPYS AND THE ROYAL COURT DISCOVER TEA

In a simply stated manner, Samuel Pepys, eminent diarist, Clerk of the
Acts to the Navy Board (rising later to become secretary of the admiralty)
and twenty-seven at the time, mentioned tea for the first time in his diary
on September 25, 1660. His day had begun at the office with a meeting
of colleagues, during which "we talked together of the interest of this
kingdom to have a peace with Spain and a war with France and Holland.
And afterwards did send for a Cupp of Tee (a China drink) of which I
never had drunk before and went away."

Seven years later his wife apparently took her first cup. His entry of
June 29 reads: "Home and found my wife making of tea; a drink which
Mr. Pelling, the poticary, tells her is good for her cold and defluxions."
Shades of Garway.

Though tea had begun to take its place in the coffee houses, it was still
a novelty, the real impetus to its popularity occurring with the marriage
of Charles II to the Portuguese Princess Catherine de Braganza in 1662.
Tea-drinking was already an established custom among the royals and
nobility of Portugal when the princess arrived in England, bringing with
her a dowry that included Tangier and Bombay and some rare teas for
court use.

At first appalled by the replacing of wines and spirits with a nonintoxicating beverage at court functions, the ladies and gentlemen of the court soon found they enjoyed it. But until the East India Company began to realize the commercial value of tea and began importing it on a regular basis in 1669, tea that was bought came from the coffee houses which had secured it through Dutch contacts or through friends with similar connections.

A year after Catherine came to England, tea was eulogized for the first time in verse. The occasion was her birthday and the poem, written by Edmund Waller, a Cavalier poet of little consequence, and entitled "Of Tea Commended by Her Majesty," treacled thusly:

> Venus Her Myrtle, Phoebus has his bays;
> Tea both excels which she vouchsafes to praise.
> The best of Queens and best of herbes we owe
> To that proud nation which the way did show
> To the fair region where the sun does rise;
> Whose rich productions we so justly prize.
> The Muse's friend, Tea, does our fancy aid,
> Repress those vapours which the head invade,
> And keep that palace of the soul serene,
> Fit on her birthday to salute the Queen.

There is no record that the Queen ever "saluted" the poet in return. Certainly, he never became the poet laureate either of the nation or the tea merchants. In short, both he and his poem were soon forgotten.

In 1666, the royal court's secretary of state, Henry Bennet, Lord Arlington, and his friend Thomas Butler, Earl of Ossory, returned from travels through the Netherlands with packets of tea stuffed in their bags. While guests in the homes of Holland's prominent citizens, they had seen in what high regard the Dutch held the drinking of tea, with every leading hostess worth her reputation pouring tea in a room set aside solely for that purpose. It was a custom they planned to promote at home, a custom similar to that in Japan but minus the formality and symbols. Some of the tea they sold for a handsome sum (more than two pounds per pound) to friends, the rest they gave to their wives. The influence their news brought was considerable and tea-drinking in England acquired a further boost to its reputation as a social entertainment among those who could afford it.

TOKENS AND TAXES

Wars have to be paid for, a fact no one likes to face and which many try to avoid. The treasury was sorely depleted during the Civil War and money was scarce when it ended in 1649. When the Commonwealth, newly created under Oliver Cromwell, found itself short of money but long on demands for payment, it assessed the wealthy tradesmen and merchants heavily—when it didn't confiscate their riches outright. Though there was a need for coins of smaller value, they didn't exist and the government had no intention of spending money to mint them. So local merchants struck their own, each one printed with the name, address and trade of its issuer, plus the redeemable value. They were not particularly impressive, artistically, but then, that was not the intent. A few were made of leather, the majority of pewter, copper or brass, and all were accepted for payment at coffee houses and shops within the immediate area. There was not much that the government could do about it—unless it minted its own—so it did nothing until 1660.

There is a great deal of poetry and fine sentiment in a chest of tea.

RALPH WALDO EMERSON (1803–1882)
Letters and Social Aims

It is axiomatic that when something is popular, a wise government will tax it, barren coffers or no. In 1660, an excise tax of eight pence per gallon was levied on every order for tea and chocolate sold in the coffee houses. If the idea was good in principle, in practice it proved costly.

Tea was initially mixed by the coffee house keeper who would then pour it into a keg, drawing upon it with each order as he did with orders for ale. Excise officers were required to visit the houses periodically, measure the amount of tea in the keg and remeasure the amount on their next visit. However, smart keepers made up enough tea to more than cover customers' needs between the visits, and hid the excess until the barrel began to empty. Then they filled it—not to the top, of course, but enough to save them both the tax and the fine (five pounds each month) for avoiding the tax.

The tax was soon scrapped but with the arrival of William of Orange to the throne in 1689, tea enthusiasts were in greater trouble. The excise tax returned, this time five shillings levied on every pound of dried tea. For a time during the enlightened 1720s, all import duties were lifted on tea, coffee and chocolate but by mid-century they were back. True, the tax was lower, but now it was topped with an *ad valorem* tax that began at 25 percent of tea's true value and rose steadily until, in 1784, it was 120 percent. Oh, how that chilled the hearts (and the hearths) of tea lovers everywhere, bringing grief as easily to the hostess in Grosvenor Square as it did to the farmer on the Downs.

Yes. Tea, the treasured drink at court, the nectar of the coffee house, the proud indulgence of the rich and fashionable, had by the 1730s made its way into the home and on to the daily table of *common man*. True, his tea was not served from fine china. Neither had it cost him a mere tuppence per pound. He paid dearly for it but, with the introduction of green tea to England a few years earlier, it was a more affordable luxury than the previously sold Bohea, or black tea, especially when he didn't have to pay the tax.

To say that all but a few Englishmen were reluctant to embark on the smuggling of tea, either for monetary profit or palatable pleasure, would be to insult the ingenuity, hard work, risks and spirit of the many who were involved. The fervor of their pursuit was both contagious and boundless, cutting through class, community, property and profession. It was no more unusual for a non-tea drinker to act as coastal lookout than it was for a rector to offer the relative safety of his church for contraband sanctuary. Principle was the banner they carried in common.

For others, of course, money was the principal pull—if not the only one—a fact which caused a pronounced labor shortage on the farms of southern England. More money could be earned in a week as a tea courier than as a field hand. So expert and swift did many of these young men become in their new vocations, they dazzled the minds of their employers as well as the revenue officers determined to run them down.

Left, "Death of Wolfe." Transfer printed Queen's Ware teapot. Impressed Wedgwood. C. 1770–1775. Right, Queen's Ware Teapot with Chinoiserie design. Hand enameled at the Chelsea workshop of Wedgwood. C. 1760. *Josiah Wedgwood & Sons, Ltd.*

A veritable network of tea routes fanned out from the coves, coveys and inlets along England's southern coast, most of them in Dorset, Cornwall and Kent. They became the hiding places for armadas of small boats returning from mid-of-night rendezvous with ships—most of them Dutch—lying at anchor a few miles off shore, their holds laden with contraband tea, tobacco, silk and brandy.

Once the goods were ashore, they were dispersed to various hiding places

nearby—into church crypts, underneath homes, to castles (two thousand pounds of tea was confiscated in one day from Hurstmonceux Castle) and into caves. Some of the caves were enlarged and ventilated ingeniously by the smugglers who then linked them up through newly created or little-used underground passages. One cave, tucked in Portcothan Bay, never was discovered by government officials, even though they crossed and recrossed the area countless times, knowing that it did exist somewhere.

Couriers alone on horseback or as part of a caravan, with tea stuffed in pouches or lining their clothes, clattered through silent villages at night. Awakened residents would await anxiously for the sound of further hoof-beats to follow, knowing then that the chase was on. They did all that they could to impede or prevent revenue officers in their pursuits, but in spite of the fierce loyalty and support they gave the smugglers, there were reverses. Some runners were caught, although not with the frequency and competency that one might expect from highly trained officials, blood was shed and contraband taken.

However, captured goods were also retrieved and with astonishing success. It was not unusual for a band of men (fifty or sixty in number, if need be) to mount a full-scale raid on a locked custom house and empty it entirely of its contents. How often they received help from the custodians inside only can be left to musing. No one ever stood up to be counted.

Most of the smugglers caught alive were shipped off to the navy where they created another reputation by serving in an exemplary manner. Those who died on behalf of tea or some other contraband were usually blanketed with a mantle of martyrdom, deserved or not. The headstone of one Robert Trotman, felled by a bullet on 24 March 1765, while unloading tea, tells it well:

> A little tea; one leaf I did not steal.
> For guiltless bloodshed I to God appeal.
> Put tea in one scale, human blood in t'other,
> An think what 'tis to slay a harmless brother.
> Lord, pardon the offender who
> My precious blood did shed;
> Grant him to rest, and forgive me
> All I have done amiss;
> And that I may be rewarded
> With everlasting bliss.

It is all very well to lump smugglers together as a rough-coated lot, no more than thieves and knaves who would as easily cut a throat as pack a pouch of tea. But such thinking does injustice to the smuggler who, while perhaps more subtle and silent in approach, achieves the same end. Mrs. Elizabeth Montague, a London woman of considerable virtue and wealth, did not row out to a waiting ship. She simply wrote her sister-in-law in Paris for tea, for lace and for other luxuries heavily endowed with taxes. Her only worry in one letter, written in 1772, was that too much contraband should not be packed in one box. "Smuggling," she wisely observed, "is a dangerous trade."

Jaspes tray,
Brewster-shaped
teapot. Sugar,
creamer, teacup,
and saucer. White
on pale blue
Jasper, with
"somestic employ-
ment" designs by
Lady Templeton.
*Josiah Wedgwood
& Sons, Ltd.*

Five years later she was more audacious in her requests. At that time, her relative was living on the English coast. "You may get me a couple of pounds of good smuggled tea at Margate, and send it to London. After I have paid you for it, I shall drink it with a safe conscience." Later: "I am told that in Paris there are waddlings for petticoats and cloaks at only a few shillings. If you could get as much as would line a cloak and quilted petticoat, it would be of great service to me; and to salve the delicacy of your conscience, I do not ask for the silk covering. Your maid may run them into her petticoat, over the lining." How thoughtful.

Mrs. Montague was hardly alone in her class with enterprising—but illicit—undertakings. A certain hypocrisy permeated government and social circles. Officials thought nothing of buying or drinking contraband tea and, of the ships not flying Dutch flags, several bringing in smuggled goods, some were owned by members of the aristocracy, well aware of their missions but with an eye to making more money.

How successful the smugglers were in their deliverance of tea is best shown by summing up the annual tea imports. Of the three hundred thousand pounds that came in during one year at the start of the eighteenth century, of the one million pounds landed in England fifteen years later, and of more than that by 1723, estimates credit the smugglers with 50 percent of all tea imported. A few in a position to know whereof they spoke were even more generous, granting the smugglers two-thirds of the imports to one-third for the East India Company.

Whatever the actual figures, it was apparent that the government was being bested at nearly every turn. However, the government moved with the speed of molasses running uphill on a windless day. Not until 1784 was the Commutation Act proposed and passed, cutting the *ad valorem* from 120 percent to 12½ percent of tea's value. This immediately canceled the need for continued smuggling and, under legal aegis, tea imports doubled.

BARBS AND BOUQUETS

Oh, how they flew, as many barbs as bouquets and all of them tossed at tea. The passion, the fervor, the contempt, the adoration, the claims, the verbiage issued on behalf of that innocent liquid were extraordinary at the least. One could claim that it all began with the Garway broadside extreme, but the first published salute to tea took the form of an advertisement two years earlier.

It appeared in *Mercurius Politicus*, a weekly described under its masthead as "comprising the sum of Forein [sic] Intelligence, with Affairs now on foot in the Three Nations of England, Scotland, & Ireland, For Information of the People." The advertisement appeared in the issue for Thursday, September 23, to Thursday, September 30, 1658, and followed the first advertisement of the week which requested information leading to the recovery of a Brightbay gelding apparently stolen by "a young man with gray cloaths [sic] of about twenty ears of age [and] middle stature."

The tea advertisement which covered three lines announced: "That Excellent and by all Physitians [sic] approved *China* Drink, called by the *Chineans, Tcha*, by other Nations *Tay alias Tee*, is sold at the Sultanessehead Cophee House in Sweetings Rents, by the Royal Exchange, London." The Sultanesse-head had been one of the very first houses to sell tea.

Less than twenty years later, the coffee houses would be termed "nurseries of idleness and pragmaticalness" and the royal proclamation for their suppression would follow. The official barb, putting down the houses as readily as their patrons, reads in part:

> Whereas it is most apparent that the multitudes of coffee houses of late years set up and kept within this kingdom, the dominion of Wales, and town of Berwick-upon-Tweed,* and the great resort of idle and disaffected persons to them, have produced very evil and dangerous effects; as well for that many tradesmen and other, do herein misspend much of their time, which and probably would be employed in and about their Lawful Calling and Affairs. . . .

Time misspent or not, teacups continued to be filled without further reproach until 1678, when young Henry Sayville sought fit to launch what

---

* Berwick-upon-Tweed was singled out because the border town between Scotland and England had belonged either to one or the other thirteen times in three hundred years until Edward IV claimed it finally for England. Only in 1885 did it officially become part of England.

was to be the first of numerous verbal assaults against tea and/or those who drank it. All of the attacks were rooted, in part or in whole, in the pits of class distinction, male superiority or religious wisdom.

In a letter to his uncle, then serving as secretary coventry to the crown, the highly displeased Sayville chastised his friends "who call for tea instead of pipes and a bottle after dinner." The habit was, he termed, nothing less than "a base Indian practise." One can only wonder how Richard Addison might have rejoined the misanthropic Sayville had he been writing for the *Spectator* at the time. But Addison was only six years old when Sayville lashed out against tea drinkers and the popular daily did not make its debut until 1721. Founded by Richard Steele, a friend of Addison's, it was a counterpoint to the *Tatler*, which he had first published two years earlier. While the *Tatler* focused on political and social news and essays, the *Spectator* juggled manners with morals, morality with wit.

Writing in a March issue that first year, Addison's feeling on tea in society was plainly positive, his seriousness couched in humor:

> It was said of Socrates, that he brought philosophy down from heaven, to inhabit among men; and I shall be ambitious to have it said of me, that I have brought philosophy out of closets and libraries, schools and colleges, to dwell in clubs and assemblies, at tea-tables and in coffee houses.
>
> I would therefore in a very particular manner recommend these my speculations to all well-regulated families that set apart an hour in every morning for tea and bread and butter; and would earnestly advise them for their good to order this paper to be punctually served up, and to be looked upon as part of the tea-equipage.

Tea tables in Scotland may not have had the daily *Spectator* with which to start the mornings, but they had tea. The serving of Bohea was brought to Scotland at Holyrood Palace by the Duchess of York (wife of the man who would become James II of England, Scotland, Ireland and Wales and Berwick-upon-Tweed) following years of exile by the couple in Holland. The year was 1680. By the start of the century, tea could be found on the shelves of many Scottish shops, be they owned by greengrocers, tobacconists or jewelers, and by 1724, all—or nearly all—of Scotland was enthralled with tea.

Duncan Forbes was not. Lord president of the court of sessions in Edinburgh, and otherwise an amiable, well-respected and superbly competent jurist, he was totally blind to tea. He termed it the base for everything bad that had occurred and would occur, warning that both the health and the prosperity of the empire and its people were doomed if the sale of tea was allowed to continue.

Perhaps his fears had their foundation in the work of another Scotsman, Dr. Thomas Short, who, in 1730, had published *A Dissertation upon Tea* in which he doubted the many qualities attributed to it. It was his belief that it was a blemish upon the human body at best and was capable of producing all kinds of ailments, including a touch of the vapors. The men had their followers and, in 1744, several towns and parishes undertook to eradicate what they saw as the "tea menace." While deploring tea as an unmanly drink, they praised beer, an attitude shared by Forbes.

In his written protest to Parliament, Forbes pointed out that the preference for tea was cutting dearly into the crown's tax on ale and countermeasures were in order. He proposed that tea be taxed severely and that a law be passed limiting those *allowed* to buy it. Yes. *Allowed.* To qualify, one would need an annual income of not less than fifty pounds. How would the government check up on just who was drinking tea who should not be drinking tea? Forbes' answer was that a house-to-house search would be in order, done under the guise of visitation at tea time. Those caught with a cup of tea in their poor hand would be hauled off to prison. Fortunately for most of the nation, his ludicrous proposals were soundly beaten down by the solicitor general.

And Venus goddess of the eternal smile,
Knowing that stormy brews but ill become
Fair patterns of her beauty, hath ordained
Celestial Tea;—a fountain that can cure
The ills of passion, and can free from frowns,
And sobs, and sighs, the dissipated fair.
To her, ye fair, in adoration bow!
Whether at blushing morn, or dewey eve,
Her smoking cordials greet your fragrant board
With Hyson, or Bohea, or Congo crowned.

ROBERT FERGUSSON (1750–1774), Untitled

One hastens to contemplate how Addison's wit would have handled that in the *Spectator.* Forbes was lucky that none of his tea-drinking opposites sought to exact revenge. Otherwise, they might have been able to provide a fair case against beer, citing an incident involving Forbes as a perfect example of beer's impure influence. It seems that on the day of his mother's burial, Forbes and his pallbearers retreated to an ale house where the bereaved son hosted many rounds of beer. When the group of mourners finally lurched into the cemetery, someone realized they'd forgotten the body.

A marriage perhaps not made in Heaven but over the pyre of tea could have been that of Forbes and Dorothy Brandshaigh. Their wedding band could have been inscribed: "I take thee but I take not tea." The lady was as righteous as the man in keeping the poor from a cup of tea. When, in 1775, Mistress Bradshaigh funded an almshouse outside London, she bequeathed one limitation along with her Christian charity—no tea in the house. She would not, she said, show charity to anyone "who can afford to indulge themselves in an article so unnecessary, so expensive, so destructive of both time and health (the tea such people must drink being poison)." Amen.

Cut from the same bolt of cloth, Arthur Young—England's most prominent economist during the late 1770s—inveighed against men "making tea an article of their food, almost as much as women, labourers losing their time to come and go to the tea-table, farmer's servants even demanding tea for their breakfast!" He prophesied the same end of the road for the empire as Forbes.

Of all the unkind cuts leveled at tea, one of the most famous came from Jonas Hanway, author and London merchant. His attack might have gone relatively unnoticed had not it roused the dander of Dr. Samuel Johnson. Hanways' critique, marking tea as "pernicious to health, obstructing industry and impoverishing the nation" appeared in his *Journal of an Eight Days Journey*, published in 1756. Johnson responded with good humor in the *Literary Magazine*, describing himself as "a hardened and shameless tea-drinker, who has for many years diluted his meals with only the infusion of this fascinating plant; whose kettle has scarcely time to cool; who with tea amuses the evening, with tea solaces the midnight, and with tea welcomes the morning."

Dr. Johnson's consummate devotion to tea has been recorded well by his biographers, most notably James Boswell. The pages of his *Life of Samuel Johnson* tell of the amounts of time spent over tea (and the amounts of cups consumed) by the lexicographer at one sitting, be that in a coffee house or at home (or, preferably, at someone else's home, because Johnson was notorious as a guest who liked to stay). Johnson thought nothing of drinking ten cups at one tea serving and, in fact, once bragged that he had consumed twenty-five in a lady's home while offering less than that number in words toward a conversation.

Had Johnson been born a hundred years later, he might have found a strong ally—and, perhaps, competitor—in tea in William Ewart Gladstone, four times prime minister during the reign of Queen Victoria, who disliked him thoroughly. Gladstone bragged too about his fondness for tea. He boasted that no other member of Parliament drank as many cups of tea in one day as he. He probably was the only resident of London who went to bed every night with a hot water bottle filled with tea at his feet. The bottle was not there to keep his feet warm between chilly sheets but to drink from when his extreme passion for tea would overcome him and no one was about to prepare it.

LONDON'S FIRST TEA SHOP

A microcosm of tea's early journeys through English life can be found in the documents and ledgers held by Twinings. The first ledger is dated October 12, 1712, and subsequent pages record amounts of tea, coffee and chocolate sold, prices paid, orders for tea to be exported, etc.

Thomas Twining opened his first coffee house in 1706 in Devereux Court. The earliest public reference to its existence was made in the *London Gazette* issue of November 7 to November 11 of that year. A notice was published concerning a bankruptcy case against Sir William Moore of Battersea and all those to whom he was indebted could convene at Tom's Coffee House on November 25 to give evidence to the commissioners.

By 1714, Thomas Twining owned three coffee houses, and in 1717 the one at Devereux Court was changed in name to the Golden Lyon and became the first tea shop, frequented by women and men. A ledger for 1714 showed that a Mrs. Carter of Kent spent £17 5s. 3d. on tea and coffee in eight months while a druggist, Mr. Allan, spent nearly double that amount in only two months.

That same year a London journal had news of a new medical additive, Tinctura Amara Basilica (the Royal bitter tincture) which, if between forty and sixty drops were added to tea or coffee or wine, would be good for both infections and diseases. That same notice stated that the medicine could be bought at Tom's Coffee House in the Strand.

Love and scandal are the best sweeteners of tea.

HENRY FIELDING (1707–1754), "Love in Several Masques"

A ledger for 1735 shows that tea sales far outweighed those for coffee and chocolate. As much as 16,479 pounds of tea were sold compared to 5,274 pounds of coffee and 3,054 pounds of chocolate.

The turning point toward tea by the religious (which, with those in the medical profession had bemoaned tea) is evident in 1739 with a purchase by the archbishop of Canterbury. The ledger entry reads: "His Grace the Archbishop of Canterbury, 2 lb. Chocolate at 4/6 per lb. and 1 lb. Green Tea at 16/-per lb."

In 1955 the Borough of Stamford, London, sent Twinings a bill head of theirs which the borough had had in its files for nearly two hundred years. The Twining bill, dated 1742, showed a lion that was smiling. Business must have been good.

Twinings began exporting tea in ever increasing amounts during the second half of the eighteenth century. In 1749, a consignment of tea was dispatched to one William Buckley Esq. of St. Kitts in the West Indies. Six pounds was sent by a friend to John Russell in Lisbon a year later, and in 1754, two majors in the Royal Welsh Fusiliers were sent tea to their station in Spain.

That same year an advertisement in the *London Press* illustrated the service still performed by coffee houses to the general public. The March 4 issue entry reads: "Lost, a ring, being an amethyst, set round with small diamonds, supposed to be dropped between Grosvenor Square and the further ends of Chelsea, going under Great James' Park Wall by Pimlico. Whoever brings it to the bar of Tom's Coffee House at Devereux Court, Temple, shall have 3 guineas." The following year an ad in the *Public Advertiser* informed the reader that "an auction of books is to be held in the Haymarket and catalogues can be had from Tom's Coffee House in the Strand."

From the May 17, 1756, issue of the *Gazetteer*, a social note read: "George Frederick Handel will direct his sacred oratorio Messiah in the Chapel of the Hospital for the Maintenance of Exposed and Deserted Young Children for this charity. To prevent the chapel being crowded, men are desired to come without swords and ladies without hoops. Tickets from Twinings."

That same year, Twinings filled overseas orders for tea from Governor Pinfold in Barbados; the Governor of Boston "in New England"; and customers in Leghorn, Antigua, Cadiz and Aix-en-Provence.

Among the documents, a plaintive note was sounded in a letter written by a young schoolboy, William Dutton, to his father. The letter, dated 1765, reads: "I wish you would be so kind to let me have tea and sugar here to drink in the afternoon, without which there is no such thing as keeping company with other boys of my standing."

Between 1748 and 1768, the Twinings ledger shows 1,446 customers were regular users of Twinings tea. Of that number, 146 were titled, 163 were of the clergy, 30 were doctors, 40 were barristers, 39 were army officers and 26 were members of Parliament. Before 1748, only 9 doctors and 22 clergymen were listed on the Twining ledgers. The two professions were slow to look upon tea with less than a suspect eye.

An on-going problem during the eighteenth century was, in spite of laws passed against it between 1725 and 1767, tea adulteration. Used leaves, sawdust, gunpowder, domestic ash leaves and other substances were mixed with tea in order to meet the public's demand for green tea at a fair price.

---

*Now for the tea of our host
Now for the rollicking bun,
Now for the muffin and toast,
Now for the gay Sally Lunn!*

SIR WILLIAM SCHWENCK GILBERT (1836–1911), *The Sorcerer*

In 1777, the Tea Adulteration Act underscored "the injury and destruction of great quantities of timber, wood and underwoods (to provide the sawdust), the prejudice of the health of His Majesty's subjects, the diminution of the revenue, the ruin of the fair trader" and "the encouragement of idleness." Still it continued, leading Thomas Twining's grandson, Richard, to issue a pamphlet in 1785 warning its readers on how "smouch" was mixed. (It took another hundred years and the passage of the English Food and Drug Act before England really saw the end of adulterated tea.)

Tea mixing—good teas blended together—was described by Richard Twining in another pamphlet:

In my grandfather's time, it was the custom for ladies and gentlemen to come to the shop and to order their own teas. The chests used to be spread out, and when my grandfather had mixed some of them together in the presence of his customers, they used to taste the tea, and the mixing was varied till it suited the palates of the purchasers. At that time, no person would have liked the tea if it had not been mixed.

When tea's reputation and sales suffered another relapse in 1792 because of high sugar prices, the tea brokers held a conference. A press cutting from the Twinings scrapbook summarizes the proceedings:

In consequence of an application from the tea brokers, a conference took place yesterday between them and the Directors of the [tea] Sale Room. Mr. Twining [Richard I] stated the fears of the trade that unless some immediate steps were taken for the reduction of the present high price of sugar, the Company's sales would be materially injured. People, he said, were leaving off tea as well as sugar. Hysons, which sold at the last sale for 6 shillings were now brought for 4 shillings 8 pence. He concluded by earnestly entreating the gentlemen behind the bar to represent their well-grounded apprehensions to His Majesty's Ministers.

Do Katydids drink tea?

OLIVER WENDELL HOLMES (1809–1894), "To an Insect"

In 1796, a chance to have tea with George Washington was turned down by Richard's brother, Thomas. In his diary he described the events leading to the invitation and the step taken which he regretted all his life. On his way home from India and service in the East India Company's Bengal Service, he visited America and journeyed to Alexandria, where he was received by the Washingtons. While talking to Mrs. Washington and her granddaughter ". . . the door opened and Mrs. Washington and myself rising, she said, 'The President' and introduced me to him. Never did I feel more interest than at this moment, when I saw the tall, upright, venerable figure of this great man advancing towards me to take me by the hand." After discussing India and trade talks then under way between that country and America, the American president asked the Englishman to take tea. The latter declined because of previous plans. His total remorse is evident in the diary entry for that day: "No engagement should have prevented me accepting such an invitation. This was one of the most memorable days. The moment when the great Washington entered the room and Mrs. Washington said, 'The President,' made an impression on my mind which no subsequent years can efface."

In 1829, the will of Thomas Rasleigh of Blackheath, Kent, showed that he had bequeathed to "Mrs. Parry, mother of my two female servants, my two brown china jars in my study filled with tea from Twinings such as I drink myself."

In 1837, Twinings received a Royal Warrant from Queen Victoria establishing the fact that it was patronized by Her Majesty's household. In effect, the Warrant also gave Twinings permission to advertise her patronage—in good taste, of course. A facsimile of the queen's coat of arms could now be hung over the front door, could appear on Twining stationery with her name underneath, and be included in any print advertising. Subsequent rulers and members of the royal family of England and other countries have confirmed their patronage by permitting their coats of arms to be used.

THE HONORABLE MONOPOLY

*Suite of bone
china teaware.
Broad platinum
band with gilded
decoration. Old
oval shape with
new Bute-shaped
teacup and saucer.
Spade, 1806.
Spade Museum,
Stoke-on-Trent,
England.*

This chapter could not end without a profile of the East India Company, whose singular power dominated the tea market and its development and, in turn, was developed through tea. On December 31, 1600, Queen Elizabeth granted a group of individual merchants a fifteen-year monopoly on trade in the East Indies. The charter was in response to a petition of theirs to develop the sea route just opened around Africa's Cape of Good Hope. The merchants had been with the Levant Company, amassing huge sums of money through their overland trade route to India. With the sea route making the Far East more accessible, these wise men foresaw the distinct advantage its development could have on British commerce (and to their own purses, of course).

Suite of bone china teaware. Spade's 557 pattern bat-printed in gray with gilded bands, lines, and decorations. New oval shape with Bute-shaped teacup. *Spade Museum, Stoke-on-Trent, England.*

Granted to the group under the title of "The Governor and Company of Merchants of London trading in the East Indies," the charter granted the Company permission to take out British currency from the country (heretofore forbidden) and to be free of import duties on its first four voyages. With new charter revisions over the next two centuries, the Company was granted extraordinary powers, making it a virtual empire unto itself. Under later charters, John Company (the name by which it was known at home) could make by-laws, coin British currency, export foreign money, conduct wars and negotiate peace, inflict penalties and punishments, be exempt from import duties on numerous goods and represent Britain as sole authority on foreign soil.

At first the Company concentrated on the rich spice market of the Netherlands Indies rather than head for India itself. With the Portuguese and Dutch East India companies firmly established in the Far East (though founded a few years after John Company), England needed to catch up quickly or perhaps be forever out of focus there. Company records show that the directors were aware of tea and the Dutch involvement in marketing China tea during the early 1600s, but they preferred importing China silks. Not until 1718 did tea displace silk as the Company's favorite article of trade.

The first tea—143 pounds worth—bought by Company factors in 1669, came from junks anchored in Bantam waters and from Portuguese ships on the Macao-Goa-Daman route. Though the first East Indiaman (as the Company ships were called) had managed to push its way past the Portuguese foothold in Macao and up the Canton River in 1637, full trading with China did not begin until 1654. That year a treaty signed by Oliver Cromwell and King John IV of Portugal opened up free entry to all ports in the East Indies.

John Company prospered during the seventeenth century as it continued to gather strength in the Far East. But at home, the crown was in need of money and toward the end of the century it sanctioned another East India Company. Cutthroat competition ensued, threatening to kill them both, and after a few years of rivalry, the companies merged.

In 1773, the Company charter was revised, granting the Company a complete monopoly on all China trade as well as India. The total control extended to China tea, allowing the Company to set the price on tea and just how much tea would be made available for sale. However, 1773 turned out to be a bad year financially for John Company. More than seventeen million pounds of tea were lodged in its warehouses, destined for the American market, but unsold. America objected to the harsh taxes imposed on tea and made her point felt when she turned to the Dutch market for its teas. To offset its growing debt, the Company asked for and received special privileges from the crown. It would be allowed to export tea, duty-free, to America, where it would be sold by Company-chosen factors who would pay the import tax rejected by the Americans. (How *they* fared is covered in the next chapter.)

In 1785, the tea dealers, headed by Richard Twining, petitioned the Crown for an end to the tea taxation which was based on the arbitrary prices set by the Company. The rage against monopolistic behavior in America had not been lost on the crown, and it agreed to end John Company's exclusive trade. According to the papers drawn up between the crown and the East India Company, three years notice of termination of the charter was mandatory. But more than three years later the monopoly was still in force. England had other problems commanding her attention,

Suite of bone china teaware. Painted in blue and red with richly gilded ornamentation in the Imari style. Octagon shape with London-shaped teacup and saucer. Spade, 1815– 1818. *Spade Museum, Stoke-on-Trent, England.*

namely Napoleon, who was trying to sever her trade completely with Europe. It was not until after the War of 1812 that the Company's monopoly in India ended and not until 1833 that she lost her singular ties with China.

It was just as well. By then, America was involved directly with trade to the Far East and, within a few years, her new ship designs would put the pride of Britain to shame on the high seas. The East Indiamen would not be a match for the pioneer clipper ships.

With the end of the Company monopoly, her ships dispersed, some of them sailing again to the Far East but under the flag of independent owners; 258 years after its founding, the reign of John Company was completely over, including its absolute rule in India.

5

Tea and America's Independence

WHO INTRODUCED TEA to the New World? Pose that question to anyone and chances are, thirteen to one, the answer will be in the manner of "Why, the English of course."

The English? It's a logical answer. After all, is not the teapot the first item packed and unpacked whenever the English move? (That is the rumor!) However, in this instance they cannot take credit for ushering in the spirit of tea to the New World. By 1669 when John Company was finally persuaded to ship regular consignments of tea to England, the favored new drink in the Netherlands had caught the fancy of the Dutch settled in New Amsterdam. There is no document in evidence which can pinpoint the very first time a cup of tea was sipped on New World soil, but historical estimates place it around the middle of the century or within ten years of having become fashionable in Holland.

Like their counterparts in the mother country, the ladies of New Amsterdam were very serious about tea and its equipage. The tea table was never set without the complete service which, at that time, consisted of teapot, hot water pot, sugar bowl and tongs, strainer, cups, saucers and spoons. (It would be left to the French to add the creamer.) One pot of tea was never enough. To please individual tastes, at least two, and usually three, different teas were ready to be poured.

It was not until 1670 that the colonial English in Boston first became aware of tea—and even then only among a limited group—and not until 1690 that tea was first sold there publicly under license (as in England). Here, too, the women cherished their tea services, to the point that it became quite the custom for the Boston ladies to carry their own cup, saucer and teaspoon to all social gatherings.

After the English captured New Amsterdam in 1674 and renamed it New York, they began adapting some of the social habits of London to their newest possession. During the first half of the nineteenth century, the tea garden was one of them. The gardens had blossomed on the outskirts of London in the early 1800s, outgrowths of the "pleasure gardens" frequented during the previous century and, by all accounts, far more pleasurable. The tea gardens were enjoyed as much by women as by men, as much by families as by couples, and, while some fashioned themselves as a playground for the wealthy, most welcomed the general public and only a very few charged admission.

Tea, coffee, hot chocolate and light foods could be bought in the gardens any hour of the day and consumed anywhere—under a tree, by a pond, taken at the side of a landscaped path, thus initiating the novelty toward outdoor eating. The season for the gardens usually ran from May until early September and visitors could take in concerts, watch fireworks, pantomimes and other entertainment, bowl, skittle, dance at one or two, or stroll through the sculptured grounds.

Sugar, coffee urn, teapot, and stand by Paul Revere. *Museum of Fine Arts, Boston, Massachusetts.*

A number of New York gardens were created around springs, with water pumps installed to make the good water available for tea (notoriously bad-tasting water prevailed in New York at the time). Among the better known of these gardens was the Tea Water Pump Garden in lower New York at the corner of Roosevelt and Chatham (later, Park Row streets). This garden's water was considered to be the best from all the springs and was sold throughout New York, bought by the barrel and the bottle from carts pushed by hawkers crying out: "Get your tea water!"

New World enthusiasm for tea continued strongest in the middle provinces and in New England, and chiefly in the more cosmopolitan towns. General acceptance was slow to come until the 1720s, when chests of tea became regular items on import manifests from John Company. By mid-century, the tea picture would change altogether, in texture and in shading, as the drink became a symbol on both sides of the Atlantic and the influence of that symbol began its extraordinary journey into the political future of America.

By mid-century, tea consumption swept the colonies, becoming particularly popular among the women, and even drunk by Indians when they could get no ale. Tea trade was highly profitable for a small number of merchants clustered in the three major ports—Boston, New York and Philadelphia—who vied with each other for control of tea sales to the rest of the colonies. Smuggling took on dimensions that equalled and, on occasion, surpassed the audacious activities rampant in England.

The flow of contraband tea into the colonies was hardly kept a secret from government officials and customs officers. But the proficiency and the wizardry under which it was accomplished appears to have numbed those in authority, rendering many impotent of action stronger than verbal affirmation of the situation. In 1752, New York's Governor George Clinton

Teapot and sugar bowl by Jacob Hurd. *Museum of Fine Arts, Boston, Massachusetts.*

Silver teapot and stand. Simeon A. Bayley, fl. 1785–1897. Initialed "EMD" for Edward and Mary (Elsworth) Dunscombe, married 1/87. *Museum of the City of New York. Gift of George Elsworth Dunscombe.*

noted that far more tea was being consumed in the northern colonies than annual import figures would indicate. An astute observation. Tea consumption was on the increase, yet John Company's ledger for that year shows 34,734 pounds of tea was landed at New York harbor, a drop of nearly half the previous year's total. (Three years later the import figure would fall to its lowest sum—sixty-one pounds—before rising again.)

Clinton's successor, George Hardy, described smuggling as being "in a flourishing state," an assessment concurred in by John Kidd of Philadelphia, who estimated that of the four hundred tea chests unloaded there in 1755–56, only sixteen arrived legally. Massachusetts' royal governor, Francis Bernard, could but bemoan the action prevalent in his jurisdiction. Writing to the Earl of Halifax in 1764, he assumed that the carts and wagons heard rumbling through empty streets at night must surely be heavy with smuggled goods.

Indeed they were, much of it tea, and much to the consternation of merchants doing business legally. Why was smuggling so consistently successful? Impetus emerged from many corners, beginning with the New World's thirst for tea, its resentment toward the high taxes placed on tea, and the availability of tea from Amsterdam, Bordeaux, Hamburg, Lisbon and other ports at wholesale prices lower than those of John Company. Smugglers were further abetted by low-paid customs officers, disgruntled government workers (they always surface) and even the honest tea merchant who liked the idea of being able to turn a higher profit on some of his tea sales.

Smuggling continued apace while John Company directors fumed, saw their own profits wilt and pleaded with Parliament to do something lest they be packed out completely. Their warehouses were overstocked with unsold tea. Finally the British government had the foresight—or was it hindsight?—to pass the Indemnity Act in July 1767, which, among other things, repealed all customs duties on teas landing in England but to be shipped to America. The act had the desired effect. Tea prices dropped, smugglers lost their edge, legal tea sales shot up, and John Company recouped some of its losses and, undoubtedly, some of its pride. Contentment reigned on both sides of the Atlantic—for the moment. Parliament had passed another act a month earlier, the Townshend Act, which was destined to produce devastating consequences.

REVOLT IN THREE ACTS

That tea became the cause célèbre in pursuit of America's independence was wholly accidental. Historic circumstances pruned the way. With the end of the Seven Years War in 1763, a series of battles was fought around the world to determine England's supremacy over France or vice versa (as it turned out, it was not vice versa). England felt America should absorb some of the cost. After all, she had had the protection of the British forces. But she had also contributed both in arms and in money, a fact acknowledged by Parliament when it repaid her some of that money. And, as pointed out by Benjamin Franklin, the colonists had "raised, paid and clothed nearly 25,000 men . . . a number equal to those sent from Great Britain, and far beyond their proportion. They went deeply into debt to do this; and all their estates and taxes are mortgaged for many years to come for discharging their debt."

It seems in some cases kind nature hath planned
That names with their callings agree,
For Twining the tea-man that lives in the Strand,
Would be "wining" deprived of his T.

THEODORE HOOK (1778–1841), Epigram

It made no difference. Britain was in need of funds and, in the opinion of Charles Townshend, first lord of trade, America was in need of being brought back into line. She was becoming too independent. Accordingly, a series of Declaratory Resolves was introduced into the House of Commons in 1764. George Grenville, prime minister, said that in a year's time the colonies would be assessed on all paper used. This meant that a tax, varying from three pence to ten pounds, would be levied on newspapers, tavern licenses, legal documents, marriage licenses, docking papers, etc. The colo-

Silver tea set. Peter de Riemer, fl. 1763–1796. Engraved with Van Rensselaer crest over "PSVR" for Philip Schuyler Van Rensselaer. *Museum of the City of New York. Gift of Mrs. Francis P. Garvan.*

nies repudiated the idea of being taxed without representation, but the principle was lost on Parliament, which dismissed alternatives proposed and passed the Stamp Act.

Although passed in England, the act was rejected in America. Packages of stamps were tossed in the waters (a hint of further things to follow?), documents were drawn up unstamped, a skull and crossbones appeared on newspapers where the stamp should have been, stamp officials quit under mob pressure and American merchants refused to buy English goods. The colonists took to wearing homespun and the English took back the Stamp Act six months later.

Townshend, however, was not to be thwarted in his conviction that America must be brought to the wall—no matter that the colonies had demonstrated quite clearly their ability to resist any wall of any material. Also ignoring the fact that Americans were taxed through laws enacted by their own legislatures, he used his new appointment as chancellor of the exchequer to push the Townshend Act through Parliament in June 1767. New revenues from the colonies would come in the form of duties. Duties on paint, lead, glass and paper; on wine, oil and fruit imported directly to America from Spain or Portugal; and, of course, on tea. Dear tea. Money raised thusly would pay the salaries of the royal governors and court-appointed justices. The act also specified that the crown could appoint a general civil list in each colony which would be responsible only to the crown, thus subverting self-government within the colonies.

"I expect to be dismissed for my pains," was Townshend's assessment of his brash behavior. But the one man who could have roused such opposition to him—William Pitt, Earl of Chatham—was too sick to do anything. Townshend wasn't sacked, but he was dismissed in another way. Three months after the passage of his bill, he was dead of fever.

Had he not died then, Townshend might have succumbed to apoplexy over the American reaction to his three pence tea tax. It sent the Americans once again over his wall and straight to Holland for tea. And once again John Company was in trouble. A year after the despised act was in force, the colonies drew up one of their own—the Nonimportation Agreement followed by a "Buy American" campaign. The obvious impact of both measures caused the English to reconsider anew the Townshend duties. In 1770, Lord Frederick North, who had succeeded Townshend as first lord of the treasury, became prime minister and repealed all of the duties except the one on tea. His reasoning was that it was the only one to bring anything of consequence into the royal coffers—all of four hundred pounds a year—and tea was the one item the colonists adored but could not reproduce on their own. (In Philadelphia, the Quakers had done very nicely manufacturing their own china, thus forcing John Company to lower prices on its china imports.)

By 1773, the Company was deep in trouble—in debt, out of cash, in disfavor with stockholders (stock value went from 280 to 160), and in a mess internally. In turn, England was in trouble. She was in danger of losing the four hundred thousand pounds the Company paid annually after all duties on tea to be exported to America were lifted in 1767, and she was in peril of losing control of the India trade should the Company collapse. What to do? Lord North took the only steps he thought would lead to the Company's survival and its place in American trade. He introduced a new bill to Parliament.

Under the Tea Act of 1773, Lord North retained the three pence tax on tea (against Company advice and American principle); voided the Company's annual 400,000 payment forever; lent it £1,400,000; and gave it permission to sell tea direct to America. This last generosity bypassed further need of the middleman in England who normally bought the teas

Silver tea set. N. Taylor & Co., fl. New York 1808–1817. Engraved "The Citizens of New York to Capt. Samuel C. Reid." *Museum of the City of New York. Bequest of Gabrielle de Cesnola Delcambre, granddaughter of Captain Reid.*

at Company auctions and sold them to America. It also bypassed free enterprise in the colonies, although that was not the intent. But with the Company free to sell direct, it could pick to whom it would sell, and it did. A small group of dealers became the consignees of Company tea which was to be sold to other American merchants. This smacked of a monopoly to the colonists, one which, if allowed to be implemented, could set a precedence for future market constriction. While it was true that the price of tea was now lower than anything the smugglers could quote, cheap tea was hardly a substitute for free trade. It was an insult.

There are few hours in life more agreeable than the hour dedicated to the ceremony known as afternoon tea.

HENRY JAMES (1843–1916), *Portrait of a Lady*

Not having seen it quite that way, the amiable but incompetent North clouded himself in the gossamer belief that all was now smooth. Both Parliament and the crown (worn by George III) were counting heavily on the American passion for tea and the American women to lead the colonies back to the tea table and Company-bought tea. With the ladies setting the example, they reasoned, even the most obstinate patriot could do little but follow. According to an article in the *Boston Evening Globe* of June 24, 1775, one patriot had accused North of trying to "damn half mankind by tempting *female weakness* with empoisoned TEA." Criticism like that must have pleased North. Both he and the king had been counting on that very weakness to determine the course Americans would take. The ladies proved him right. They did lead the way and patriots did follow—but not in any direction that would bring a smile to North, to Parliament or to the crown.

THE LADIES HAVE THEIR SAY

In early October of 1773, tea that had been stored for a long time in Company warehouses was loaded onto ships, destination America. There were 342 chests earmarked for Boston, 698 for Philadelphia and New York, and 257 for Charleston. Each shipment would be received by the appointed consignees.

Among the colonial women, momentary joy over the news turned to absolute rage when word crossed the Atlantic that the tea was old, probably had rotted, and that the English were trying to dupe tea-mad Americans into buying any kind at such a cheap price.

The men had already protested the Tea Act with petitions sent to Parliament and the king, with meetings in town halls and demonstrations. But

Teapot made by
Simeon Soumaine.
C. 1730. *Museum
of the City of New
York. Gift of
Mr. and Mrs.
Albert K.
Baragwanath.*

now the women took their steps. In Boston, between three and five hundred joined together under the banner of "Mistresses of Families" in a pledge to rid tea from their homes and tables until the tax was removed. One hundred younger Bostonian women promised never to drink tea at home or when offered to them, and children vowed to do the same—once they were old enough to have it offered them.

Tribute to the distaff side came in an editorial of the *Boston Evening Post*: "The wise and virtuous part of the Fair Sex of Boston and other Towns are sensible that by the consumption of Teas they are supporting the Commissioners and other Tools of Power. They have voluntarily agreed not to give or receive any further Entertainments of that Kind until such Creatures, together with the Boston Standing Army, are removed, and the Revenue Act repealed."

In Hartford, Providence, New York, Philadelphia, Washington, Annapolis, New Haven and other towns, women took similar pledges and the men followed suit. It became impossible to buy or be served tea without a medical permit. Anyone caught with tea in his possession was given the choice of handing it over or being handed over to the women for appropriate discipline. Exhausted after so many long nights of meetings, John Adams stopped by a tavern and asked if it were all right to buy tea that had not been taxed, but the answer was no. Tea was truly banished.

Mercy Otis Warren, Massachusetts lady, playwright, sister of James Otis (leading colonial lawyer) and hostess of a political salon, expressed her thoughts satirically in a poem to Connecticut's Governor John Winthrop:

For if 'twould save the nation from the curse
Of standing troops—or name a plague still worse,
Few can this choice, delicious draught give up,
Though all Medea's poison fill the cup.

Substitutes for the "pernicious herb" and "baneful weed" were found for the tea tables—and, surprisingly, enjoyed. Hyperion tea came from raspberry leaves, Liberty tea from the four-leafed loosestrife. Leaves of sage, ribwort, strawberries and currants also were picked, soaked and dried before becoming "tea."

TEA PARTIES OF ANOTHER SORT

Up and down the Atlantic coast, Americans held meetings and passed resolutions denouncing the Company, Parliament, tax on tea and any thought of allowing the tea to land. According to the Revenue Act, the tax was to be collected only when the tea was unloaded at American ports. Therefore, the target to be met was the prevention of the tea chests from leaving the ships.

Handbills flooded the towns, warning citizens to withstand the impending invasion of their freedom by the Company in concert with Parliament, and to exert pressure upon the consignees to resign or be considered the enemy. Committees of Correspondence were formed in each of the colonies to organize proper resistance measures. A New York newspaper, aptly named the *Alarm*, warned in October that "If you touch one grain of the accursed tea you are undone. America is threatened with worse than Egyptian slavery. . . . The language of the Revenue Act is that you have no property you can call your own; that you are vassals, the live stock, of Great Britain."

In Endymion, *I leaped headlong into the sea, and thereby have become better acquainted with the soundings, the quicksand, and the rocks, than if I had stayed upon the green shore, and piped a silly pipe, and took tea and comfortable advice.*

JOHN KEATS (1795–1821), Letters to James Hessey, 9 Oct. 1818

Very little pressure was needed for the New York consignees to resign. Even less persuasion was necessary in Philadelphia. But, in Boston, the consignees—among them, the two sons and a nephew of the highly unpopular governor of Massachusetts Bay, Thomas Hutchinson—resisted all requests, all warnings. On November 18, Samuel Adams headed a committee which once again asked the consignees to reconsider. They wouldn't

*Teas of the
World*

"The Tea Party"
by Henry Sargent.
C. 1821–25.
*Museum of Fine
Arts, Boston,
Massachusetts.
Gift of Mrs.
Horatio A. Lamb
in memory of Mr.
and Mrs. Win-
throp Sargent.*

and four days later the committees of five Massachusetts towns met in
Boston, asked for guidance from other towns in the colony, received support
from committees in other colonies and determined to take a strong stand
against the ships soon to land.

The mood, the attitude of Boston is clear in a letter written by Anne
Hulton, sister of Boston's commissioner of customs, to a friend in England.
Dated November 25, the letter tells that:

> The Ships Laden with Tea from the East India House are hourly ex-
> pected. The people will not suffer it to be landed in Boston. They demand
> the Consignees to promise to send it back. Mr. Clark resolutely refuses
> to comply, and will submit to no other terms than to put it into a ware-
> house till he can hear from England. They threaten to tear him into

pieces if it lands. He says he will be torn to pieces before he will desert the Trust reposed in him by the Consigners. His Son, who is just arrived from England, and all the family were got together the first night, rejoicing at his arrival, when the Mob surrounded the House, attacked it with stones and clubs, and did great damage to the windows and furniture . . . but Providence directed them so that they did not fall on anyone. All the avenues to the house were guarded by armed Men to prevent Mr. Clark escaping. This was beyond anything of the kind since we came here. [Not quite.]

Hutchinson was again approached to change the orders of the consignees and again he refused. On Sunday, November 28, the first of three tea-laden ships entered Boston harbor. Samuel Adams exacted a promise from the

Portrait of Paul Revere by John Singleton Copley. C. 1768–70. *Museum of Fine Arts, Boston. Gift of Joseph W. William B., and Edward H.R. Revere.*

Dartmouth's owner that the ship would not be boarded until Tuesday, and the following day (Monday), the Boston Committee of Correspondence convened with those of the five other towns and, without one opposing vote, agreed that Francis Rotch should send back his ship to England, ordered guards placed around the *Dartmouth* and forbade Rotch to board his ship or his captain to unload the tea secretly.

On Tuesday the Boston consignees sent a message to the committees promising to store the tea and not sell it until further orders came from England (this was met with boos and hisses), Hutchinson ordered the committees to disband (similar response), Rotch and his captain promised to return the tea to England and the committee passed a resolution forbidding future tea shipments to Massachusetts until the tax was repealed. Copies of the resolution were handed to each captain docking in any Massachusetts port and were sent to Parliament and to the governors of New York and Pennsylvania.

---

*O Tea! O leaves torn from the sacred bough!
  O stalk, gift born of the great gods!
What joyful region bored thee? In what part of the sky
Is the fostering earth swollen with your health, bringing increase.*

PIERRE DANIEL HUET (c. 1709), "Tea Elegy"

It was the law that any cargo must be landed within twenty days of arrival in port or else be seized by customs. Though Rotch and his captain had made their promise, the ships were still in port on December 11. His excuse? He lacked the necessary clearance papers. The governor refused to give them. So did the Custom House—unless, of course, the tea was landed first.

Nearly seven thousand people crowded into and around the Old South Meeting House on Thursday morning December 16. Hutchinson had ordered guns from the castle at harbor's edge to fire on any ship that left port without the proper papers and Rotch was not about to put his ship and crew in jeopardy. The committee ordered him to Hutchinson's to get that pass while it considered what steps to take.

By mid-afternoon there was no news from Rotch but the committee had agreed that the tea must not be landed. "Who knows," said one John Rowe, "how tea will mingle with salt water?" Not until dark did Rotch return to the Meeting House, minus the governor's pass. The news was announced and met with a profound silence. Samuel Adams stood up and said: "This meeting can do nothing more to save the country."

Those ten words signaled the end of legal measures and the start of forceable means. Legend has it that almost instantly someone in the crowd either let out a warhoop or cried, "Indians!" and fifty men, so dressed, swept past the door and down to Griffin's Wharf. By the time the crowd could make its way there, too, each of the three ships had been bordered by fifty men disguised in Indian garb and painted faces and every one of the chests of tea was cut open and their contents dumped into the harbor.

A historic marker heralds the event:

Here Formerly Stood

GRIFFIN'S WHARF

at which lay moored on Dec. 16, 1773, three British ships with cargoes of tea. To defeat King George's trivial but tyrannical tax of threepence a pound about ninety citizens of Boston partly disguised as Indians boarded the ships, threw the cargoes, three hundred and forty-two chests in all, into the sea, and made the world ring with the patriotic exploit of the

BOSTON TEA PARTY

No! ne'er was mingled such a draught
In palace, hall or arbor,
As freemen brewed and tyrants quaffed
That night in Boston Harbor.

The verse lines came from Oliver Wendell Holmes' "Ballad of the Boston Tea Party."

Who were the "Indians"? No one knows. It was a secret tightly kept, though rumor persists in claiming Samuel Adams and John Hancock two of the "chiefs."

OTHER TEA PARTIES

Four days before the Boston Tea Party, the brig *Greyhound* docked unexpectedly in Greenwich, New Jersey. On board was some of the tea originally destined for Philadelphia, but after being warned not to enter that port, the captain slipped into this one and the tea was unloaded and stored in the cellar of a man loyal to the crown. The secret was soon discovered, a meeting of Cumberland County residents was held, its decisions termed too weak by a group of young patriots who took the reign, literally and figuratively. On the night of December 22, they disguised themselves as Indians, met at a prearranged spot (they came from several towns), and, on horseback, tore through the streets to Market Square, broke into the cellar, hurled the tea and the chests into the middle of the Square and set it afire.

In the meantime, the *London* had docked at Charleston, South Carolina, with tea on board and, after two town meetings in which it was agreed that "tea ought not to be landed, received or vended in this colony; that no teas ought to be imported by any person whatever while the act imposing the unconstitutional duty remains unrepealed," the consignees agreed not to touch it. Twenty days after the ship docked, the cargo was seized by the custom house and stored without untoward incidence but, when more tea arrived on board the *Brittania Ball* on November 3, 1774, Charleston rebelled. Effigies of George III and North were strung up and the ship's captain gave his own tea party. He dumped the teas into the waters.

The day after Christmas of 1773, the captain of the *Polly* anchored his ship at Gloucester Point just outside Philadelphia—he had no choice to do otherwise. A committee of patriots intercepted it. He was told of resolutions passed in the city that included the tarring and feathering of any captain who allowed tea to leave his ship. As he was taken through the city, posters heralding this action caught his eye and he agreed that the ship would leave for England immediately after reprovisioning her.

A similar scenario was played out by the *Nancy* and her crew who, though they set sail from London the same time as the other ships, were sent far off course by bad weather and didn't reach New York until April 18, 1774. Captain Lockyear was granted permission to get supplies in New York and leave there in five days. A handbill was printed on the twenty-first, advising its readers of the captain's departure on the twenty-third and the suggestion made that everyone gather at the dock to see him off and thus show him how the city feels about the tax on tea.

The day before the *Nancy* was to weigh anchor, the *London* docked and her captain kept insisting no tea was on board. At first he was believed but then he wasn't, the ship was searched, tea was found, tea was dumped overboard and the captain got away, sneaking aboard the *Nancy* in the dark. She left port early the next morning to the sounds of cannon bursting (not at her), every church bell ringing, crowds cheering both the ship and the courteous captain, and a band giving him an extra ruffle.

In October of 1774, the *Peggy Stewart* was due to arrive in Annapolis with a consignment of tea among her cargo, two thousand pounds to be exact. A meeting of the area's leaders determined that the tea would not be allowed to land on the day the ship was due—October 19—but when it did pull in, it was learned that the tax had been paid by the ship's owner. Angry citizens converged upon his house, quickly built a gallows and then gave Anthony Stewart the option of being hung or of helping set fire to his ship. He chose the latter and returned to Scotland by other means.

THE LADIES OF EDENTON

Six days after the *Peggy Stewart* keeled over in Annapolis, fifty-one women from Edenton, North Carolina, gathered together under the leadership of the thrice-widowed Mrs. Penelope Barker and vowed to refuse "to conform to the pernicious custom of drinking Tea, until such time that all Acts which tend to enslave our Native Country shall be repealed."

They then sent a document attesting to their resolve and carrying each of the fifty-one signatures to a London newspaper. It appeared in the January 16, 1775, issue of *The Morning Chronicle & London Advertiser* and reads, in part:

> . . . many ladies of this province had determined to give a memorable proof of their patriotism, and have accordingly entered into the following honourable and spirited association, [sending] it to you to shew your fair countrywomen, how zealously and faithfully American ladies follow the laudable example of their husbands, and what opposition your matchless ministers may expect to receive from a people, thus firmly united against them.

It was of course "the talk of London" for days to come. It was also a very bold gesture for these women to have made. Tea parties were very much a part of their social life. It was not that easy to give up. But principle helped them to on October 25, 1774.

Tea chest, China. Wood. C. 1810. *Museum of the American China Trade, Milton, Massachusetts.*

Tea caddy.
Chinese, lacquer
and mother-of-
pearl. C. 1836.
*Museum of the
American China
Trade, Milton,
Massachusetts.*

Needless to say, England was appalled at the activity storming through
the colonies. Retaliation was taken where it could be—in Boston. The
charter of Massachusetts was annulled and the Boston Port Bill passed by
Parliament on March 25, 1774. On June 1, the bill became effective and
the port of Boston was forcibly closed to all shipping, all exports, all imports. England was going to bring her to the ground by starving her. Samuel
Adams and his followers, now more radical than ever, drew up a Solemn
League and Covenant which they hoped all Americans would follow by
promising neither to buy British merchandise nor to sell goods to England
until the bill was rescinded. New York and Philadelphia sought calmer
ways, the former proposing a Continental Congress be called, the latter
approving the plan. More coercive acts passed by Parliament that summer
solidified the American radical with the American moderate and the Continental Congress convened in Philadelphia on September 5, 1774.

6

Tea and India

"A DISCOVERY has been made of no less importance than that the hand of Nature has planted the shrub within the bounds of the wide dominion of Great Britain; a discovery which must materially influence the destinies of nations; it must change the employment of a vast number of individuals; it must divert the tide of commerce, and awaken to agricultural industry the dormant energies of a mighty country, whose well being must be the great aim of a paternal government."

How prophetic were those words spoken by the English doctor, G. G. Sigmond, before the Royal Medico-Botanical Society in London. The shrub in question was, of course, tea; the theme of the speech tea and its medicinal and moral effects; the year, 1839, shortly after the first eight chests of native India tea were sold at auction in London. The date of the auction was January 10, sixteen years after the bush was first discovered growing wild in India, fourteen years after London encouraged individual development of tea in India, and five years after India's Tea Committee was founded to pursue that development.

History was made January 10 for another reason. During eleven of those sixteen years, the English in Calcutta were consistent in their failure to acknowledge existence of the native jat, even though time and again examples of its presence were made evident. When the studied indifference finally was replaced by reluctant acceptance, collective enthusiasm was such that had any native plant been dependent upon it for life support, it would have withered within the day. The English clung to the Chinese jat as the superior one. The Indian bush would serve merely as a signpost, signaling that wherever it grew so could grow the Chinese plant. And better. How wrong they were.

EARLIER RECOGNITIONS

The natives of India were not so foolish. They had been familiar with the wild plant for many, many years, using it first to create a vegetable food called *miang*, something akin to pickled tea, and then to make a thick soup similar in texture to the notorious-tasting yak butter tea of Tibet. Recognition of tea as a drink in India appears in two travel books published during the seventeenth century. In Olearius's collection, *Description of Journeys in Muskovy and Persia,* Johan von Mandelslo wrote that at the daily meetings he attended ". . . we took only *The* which is commonly used all over the Indies, not only among those of the country, but also among the Dutch and the English who take it as a drug." John Ovington's *Voyage to Suratt* echoed Mandelslo's observations.

Though the East India Company had established three trading posts in India during the seventeenth century, its full investment in the country did not surface until a century later when, in 1757, Robert Clive, the Company's governor of Fort St. David, defeated the nawab of Bengal in two impressive battles and routed French attempts to unseat British control. With his victories, British sovereignty over all of India began and, in 1763, was recognized formally in the Treaty of Paris.

So hear it then, my Rennie dear,
Nor hear it with a frown;
You cannot make the tea so fast
As I can gulp it down.

I therefore pray thee, Rennie dear,
That thou wilt give to me
With cream and sugar softened well,
Another dish of tea.

DR. SAMUEL JOHNSON (1709–1784), Untitled

British recognition of India's native tea plant did not follow. For every step taken in its direction by individuals, British authority, abetted by John Company directors, took two backward. In 1780, Warren Hastings, Clive's successor and first governor general of India, encouraged trade with China and even sent some Chinese tea seeds to Bhutan for propagation, where they were dutifully ignored. At the same time, Colonel Robert Kyd success-

fully planted some of the same variety seeds in his own garden, watched
them grow, passed on information of his success and saw his suggestions
snubbed.

In 1788, the British naturalist Sir Joseph Banks drew up a detailed plan
on how to introduce tea cultivation into India, which the Company promptly
turned down. In 1815, a British colonel reported seeing a native tribe in
the hills of Assam take a drink made from the wild tea bush growing there.
That report was allowed to die without investigation as were several other
attempts to verify the plant's natural existence, including an experimental
tea nursery with Chinese jats begun in 1832 by a British surgeon in the
Nilgiri hills. When he died a year later, everything ended there.

DISCOVERY AND A CHALLENGE

Major Robert Bruce was finally credited with having his discovery of the
indigenous plant accepted without challenge, although technically one could
argue that credit should go to the Singpho chief who led him to it. In 1823,
the major was ordered to Assam on a trading mission and, while there,
made a number of trips into the hill district where the tea tree grew in
profusion. He made an agreement with the chief to pick up some tea
plants and seeds on his trip there the following year. But, in 1824, the
English were at war with Burma, the major was sent elsewhere and his
brother, C. A. Bruce, was posted to Assam. The plants and seeds were
delivered to him and a year later, the same year his brother died, C. A.
Bruce planted most of the seeds and plants in his own garden.

Bruce's interest in his brother's original findings led him to experiment
and cultivate the plant and, eventually, to become superintendent of tea
culture in Assam. In 1838 a book of his was published in Calcutta on the
manufacture of black tea at Suddeya in Upper Assam. An extract follows:

"The Muttuck country, which I have traversed most, appears to me to
be one vast Tea country, and I feel confident that not one half of its Tea
tracts have been yet discovered. Great numbers of the Tea tracts have been
cut down in sheer ignorance by the natives and converted into paddy fields.
I know of three tracts where the paddy had been collected and the Tea
plants had sprung up again. . . . Almost every inhabitant of the Muttuck
country knows now the Tea leaf, seeing how much we prize it, and getting
little rewards from me when they bring in a branch from any new tract.
The Singphos have known and drank the Tea for many years, but they
make it in a very different way from what the Chinese do." (Sometimes
they ate it with oil and garlic, sometimes they turned it into a bitter drink.)
"These Singphos pretend to be great judges of Tea. The Singpho country
is a fine one, but as long as the nation can get the Tea leaves from the
jungles, they never will cultivate the plant."

A challenge to cultivate the plant had been put forth in 1825 by the
English Society of Arts in London which offered a gold medal (or twenty

guineas) to the individual who would "grow and prepare the greatest quantity of tea in good quality, not being less than twenty pounds in weight, in the East or West Indies or any other British colony." The award would be made through the Agricultural and Horticultural Society in Bengal. In spite of the bid for action, John Company continued wearing its blinders until 1833, when China refused renewal of its exclusive trade agreement. Minus the security of its lucrative monopoly, the Company was left with no other choice but to turn to new worlds to explore—and exploit.

THE TEA COMMITTEE CIRCULAR

Prodded by an anxious London that the supply of tea should never be found wanting, the Tea Committee was founded in 1834 by Lord William Charles Cavendish Bentinck, governor general of India. The three original committee members, appointed in January 1834, were augmented to thirteen, two of whom were Indian. It was Lord Bentinck's intent that a plan be devised and implemented by the men to introduce tea cultivation into India.

The first cup moistens my lips and throat;
The second cup breaks my loneliness;
*The third cup searches my barren entrail but to find therein some five
    thousand volumes of odd ideographs;*
*The fourth cup raises a slight perspiration—all the wrongs of life pass
    out through my pores;*
At the fifth cup I am purified;
The sixth cup calls me to the realms of the immortals.
*The seventh cup—ah, but I could take no more! I only feel the breath
    of the cool wind that raises in my sleeves.*
*Where is Elysium? Let me ride on this sweet breeze and waft away
    thither.*

LU T'UNG (Chinese poet during T'ang Dynasty), "Tea-Drinking"

Two months after its founding, the committee sent forth its circular and its secretary. The latter was dispatched to China to study every facet of tea's cultivation and manufacture and to return with plants, seeds and experienced labor. The widely distributed circular called for information leading to the best tea-growing areas in the country. Soil, climate and topographical requisites essential to its success were described in full.

One of those whom the circular reached was Captain Francis Jenkins, agent for Assam and resident of Assam Valley, where the hills were covered with the wild plant. He wrote a report to the British government in Calcutta on the indigenous plant and sent Lieutenant Andrew Charlton into the hills for cuttings. It was Lieutenant Charlton's second contact with the native jat. In 1831 he had learned of it from the hill tribes near Sadya and sent three plants to Calcutta where they arrived in poor shape, died and were identified as plain camellias. His second shipment included leaf, fruit and blossom of the tea bush, making it impossible to identify wrongly, and samples of the leaf after it had been prepared for the native's drink.

Tho' tay is not my divarsion.

RUDYARD KIPLING (1865–1936)
Life's Handicap, "The Courting of Dinah Shadd"

Incredible as it may seem, preference for the China seed to be implanted in Indian soil persisted. A commission of two biologists and one geologist, appointed in 1835, couldn't come to terms on the best site for the experimental gardens. Two favored Upper Assam, the third opted for the Himalayas; and one insisted on using the China plants, whose centuries-old cultivation was assured, to the untried native bush. As a result, the India tea plant was little exploited until a series of failures with the China jat convinced the committee, the commission and Calcutta to pay attention to the hills of Assam and the efforts of C. A. Bruce.

With the help of Chinese labor sent him by the committee, Bruce had ranged through the vast tracts of tea plants, cut through jungles, secured the trust of sceptical natives and produced the first teas that could be made into a pleasant drink. When the shipment of India teas was auctioned on January 10, three of the chests contained Assam Souchong and five, Assam Pekoe. A second lot, totaling 95 chests of even better quality Assam, was sold at auction March 17, 1840. Put up by the British East India Company, they marked the true beginning of India teas into England and the gradual decline of China teas. (In 1836, 49 million pounds of tea reached Britain, all of it Chinese. In 1859, 69 million pounds came in, 2 million of which were from India. By century's end, the amount was 250 million pounds, of which 55 percent was Indian, 37 percent from Ceylon and 5 percent from China. In another five years, India's export alone reached 214 million pounds.)

THE GOLD MEDAL BROUHAHA

The awarding of the gold medal offered by the English Society of Arts stirred up a veritable hornet's nest of protests. Several claims had been put in for it, the first of which was submitted by Dr. Nathaniel Wallich on behalf of Lieutenant—now Captain—Charlton. Ironically, it was Dr. Wallich who, as superintendent of the Botanical Gardens in Calcutta, had dismissed the then lieutenant's first specimens of tea, sent to him in 1831, as plain camellia. Charlton's claim was passed over in favor of that entered by C. A. Bruce, who did receive the medal in recognition of his extraordinary contribution in promoting the Assam plant and that of his brother in initially finding it.

We had a kettle; we let it leak:
Our not repairing it made it worse.
We haven't had any tea for a week . . .
The bottom is out of the Universe.

RUDYARD KIPLING, "Natural Theology"

The decision pleased neither Captain Charlton nor the recently promoted Major Jenkins, and a battery of letters, claims and proofs flew between Assam and Calcutta and London. Finally convinced that their claims were valid, the Society of Arts extended the medal to both men. The presentation, made on January 3, 1842, acknowledged the captain's role in establishing full well the existence of the Assam plant and the major's efforts in pursuing the matter to this conclusion. At no time was mention ever made of Moneram Dewan, the Singpho chief who showed Robert Bruce where the wild plant grew. Appreciation of his part in the founding of India's extraordinary trade has yet to be realized.

THE PUNCTURED BALLOON

It would be delightful to report that, from 1840 on, the most pressing problem faced by the burgeoning tea industry of India was in filling all the requests piling up for the Assam teas. Truth is, almost from the start there was trouble. Deep trouble.

In March of 1840, the newly formed Assam Company, an amalgamation of two companies and with two boards of directors—one in London, the other in Calcutta—was given two-thirds of the British government's experimental tea gardens to cultivate. The gardens were given outright for a period of ten years. While approving the new monopoly, the East India Company, through one of its directors, feared that the private enterprise might prove an empty one. C. A. Bruce joined the Company as superintendent for the northern sector, Chinese labor was brought in to fill the gap of Assam workers fighting the Burmese invasion and the Calcutta board of directors' annual meeting in mid-1841 sent up an encouraging

flare. By year's end the production of cultivated tea would quadruple from
the previous year.

Also by year's end the Chinese labor had proved itself worthless—the
only thing they had in common with those working the Chinese tea gardens
was their nationality. Whoever had chosen those sent to Assam had not
looked beyond their faces. These were men who worked in bazaars, not in
tea gardens. They knew nothing about tea. Cholera added to the depletion
of competence and manpower, cutting down the white man in as great
numbers as it did the pathetic work force culled from anywhere it could
be found. And, instead of showing the estimated 40,000 pounds worth of
manufactured tea, the Company could produce only 29,000 pounds.

The pessimism expressed by the conservative director of the East India
Company was reflected in a caustic dispatch published in *Friend of India*.
Referring to the maiden voyage of a new steamer, the newspaper observed
that "the Assam Tea Company, after having sent their new steamer on one
trip up the Berhampooter, have, on her return, offered her for sale. The
cause is not made known—probably her inability to steam the Berhampooter."

Inability was the key word. The Company's London directors had cause
to worry but waited two years before sending out representatives to assess
the situation. Bruce and his southern sector counterpart were fired and the
truth was uncovered. The holdings in Assam had been completely mis-
managed, no one knew what they were doing working in the gardens or in
the tea factories, records had been falsified to document greater growth
than was real and, unless drastic steps were taken, there would soon be
nothing left to worry about. Stock value dropped, two garden groups were
closed, new managers brought in and in 1847, minus confidence from any
corner, the Company directors gave its dying enterprise one more try.

---

*So they were married—to be the more together—
And found they were never again so much together,
Divided by the morning tea,
By the evening paper,
By children and tradesmen's bills.*

LOUISE MACNEICE (1907–1963), "Les Sylphides"

Within a year, the picture had changed completely and the year-end
records actually showed a three-thousand-pounds profit. By 1852, with all
the gardens open, the Company paid its stockholders a 2½ percent divi-
dend; by 1856, it was 9 percent. The extraordinary turn-around was due
principally to three men, two of whom entered the picture in 1847, one
as deputy chairman of the Calcutta board of directors, the other as manager
of Assam. They brought to the industry new methods of cultivation, tech-
nical skill to make it succeed and a work force trimmed to 100 (well,

nearly 100) percent competency. The third man, George Williamson, entered the picture in 1853 when the other two retired. Williamson became manager of Assam and it is to him that the tea industry is beholden for insisting that the imported Chinese jat be weeded out gradually in favor of the native Assam plant.

MANIA, PANIC AND DESPAIR

Tea production began to spread into other sectors of India after the success of the second shipment of Assam teas sold at auction. The Chinese plant was brought in by the thousands and managed to do well for its growers, but when the Assam bush was found growing wild beyond the Assam borders, the trend toward planting it began to gain favor. By this time—the year was 1861—southern India was laying out its tea gardens, the northern provinces, from west to east, were filled with tea gardens, some of them privately owned.

The trend to private ownership began with the government's desire to promote tea cultivation during the early days. It was easy then to acquire vast tracts of land for very little payment. But, as the industry prospered, demand for land increased and the government was forced to invest in stricter regulations. Speculator and planter alike were required to sign 99-year leases containing many clauses by a law which became a rule in 1854, caused considerable grief and anger and had its stuffing removed through new legislation seven years later. If only London had held on. If . . .

The old philosopher is still among us in the brown coat with the metal buttons and the shirt which ought to be at the wash, blinking, puffing, rolling his head, drumming with his fingers, tearing his meat like a tiger, and swallowing his tea in oceans.

THOMAS BABINGTON MACAULEY, BARON MACAULEY (1800–1859)
Life of Johnson

If nothing succeeds like success, then it is not too outré to assume that nothing sticks closer on the heels of success than greed. It certainly appeared that way in India where every Tom, Dick and Jack-o'-knaves expected to make his fortune in tea. Each dawn saw the birth of new companies and more investors clamoring to get in at the beginning; "gardens" planted and opened without any thought to proper soil and climate conditions, let alone competent help; and existing gardens stretched beyond their capabilities. Land was sold at exorbitant prices and wrong acreage quotes; tea seeds fetched sums ridiculously beyond their worth; and labor was hired at whatever wage the individual chose to quote. The "tea mania," as history calls it, was no different from the gold fever that was soon to follow halfway round the globe. Men who, under ordinary conditions, could make rational estimates and sound judgments, were caught in a frenzy that precluded either common sense or caution. They reached the outer edges of the tea mania in 1865, clung tenaciously to their dream and saw it all drop before them.

*Oh some are fond of Spanish wine, and some are fond of French.
And some swallow tay and stuff fit only for a wench.*

JOHN MASEFIELD (1878–1967), "Captain Stratton's Fancy"

The frenzy to buy was replaced with panic to sell. Investors sold out for whatever they could get, land was available for a fraction of its true value and men were bankrupt—of money, land and friends. To London eyes the picture appeared bleak if not hopeless, but a commission sent to assess the situation in 1867 happily reported that the gardens of Assam, Sylhet and Cachar had not been blighted by the hands of greed. They were flourishing and the industry, though obviously in distress, was sound basically and would survive. By 1870, investors once again were receiving returns on their holdings.

SOME TEA-GROWING AREAS

Assam.   The sweeping plains of the Brahmaputra valley, fed by the river of the same name, contains the richest soil in the province. Both banks of the river and the climatic conditions lend themselves ideally to tea's cultivation, with more than 50 percent of all India teas produced there. Not only is Assam the largest tea-bearing region in the country, it is one of the largest in the world, with more than two million acres devoted to tea.

A fair amount of rain falls ten months of the year over all the valley, with heavy monsoon showers concentrated from August to mid-October. January and February are the dry months, March the month when the dormant bushes come to life. Cropping begins as early as March and lasts until mid-December. The tea plants are predominantly of the "Assam Indigenous" and the "Manipur Indigenous" variety, leaf color varying from light green in the former to a deeper shade in the latter.

First flush can begin in late March and last two to two and a half months or, until June, which signals the start of the *second flush* growth. Leaves of the *second flush*, considered the vintage Assam teas, are characterized by an excessive amount of silvery down called *tip* on their undersides which distinguishes the flavor and strong liquor of Assam teas from others. When fermented, the leaves show a lot of the golden *tip*.

The monsoon period accelerates nature's growth in the valley, including the tea bushes, which is why 75 percent of all Assam teas are grown then. But the *rain teas*, as the *third flush* is known, are not of the highest quality and find their way into the less expensive blends of tea. As the climate gradually becomes colder and less wet, the *autumnals*—similar in quality to the *second flush*—make their appearance. With December, the dormant period sets in.

Once manufactured, the Assam teas are sent to Calcutta for auction in the international markets and to Gauhati, a smaller auction center, for internal consumption.

---

*Whenever I sit in a high chair
For breakfast or dinner or tea,
I try to pretend that it's my chair,
And that I am a baby of three.*

A. A. MILNE (1882–1956), "Nursery Chairs, The Fourth Chair"

Darjeeling. Tucked away in the foothills of the Himalayas, in the extreme north of India, is the hill resort of Darjeeling. It is a land of incredible beauty, 7,000 feet above sea level and surrounded by masses of peaks, the tallest of which, Kanchenjunga, is over 28,000 feet. The tea gardens are laid out on the steep hillsides for many, many miles. From the air, they resemble blankets of green scallops difficult to reach on the steep, narrow, serpentine roads. Until fairly recently, pack ponies carried the plucked leaves from the distant gardens to the garden-owned factories and then the chests of tea to the railhead. Now four-wheel-drives do the job.

The Darjeeling tea is available in limited quantities. Crop yield is small per acre, the leaf is small in size and it is expensive to harvest. In fact, Darjeeling accounts for little more than 3 percent of India's total tea cultivation. It is impossible to pinpoint the exact cause for the leaf's distinct flavor. Certainly climate, soil, elevation, slow growth and type of bushes contribute to the "muscatel" that has made it the champagne of teas. But even the air breathed by the bushes is a factor. Take any one away and the results would be disappointing at best.

Most of the tea bushes belong to the China jat, China Hybrid and Hybrid Assam. The leaves are also covered with *tip* on the underside, which sometimes appears on the stalk. Though not as good a yielder as the Assam plant, the China jat does produce highly flavored teas. However, because the tea plant is excessively hybrid in nature, it is an accepted fact that no two tea bushes are alike, so that even generic propagation from seeds will yield bushes entirely different from the parent plant. As a result, every garden has been experimenting with clonal propagation, entire areas re-planted with clones from bushes much above average in quality and yielding superb results.

Darjeeling's cropping season begins in March following the first light showers after winter. This is the period of the *first flush*, which is only a degree less perfect than the *second flush*, which is gathered in May and June. Monsoons come to Darjeeling by mid-June and continue until September's end. During this time, the leaves contain a lot of moisture and are only of standard quality. While the rainfall in Assam is distributed evenly, that in Darjeeling is plentiful but scattered. The winter months are particularly dry following the plucking of another vintage tea, the *autumnals*, in October.

Manufactured tea is shipped to Calcutta auction for the international market and to Siliguri for the domestic market.

Nilgiris. Literally translated, the Nilgiris mean *Blue Mountains*, and blue they are from the haze that covers the wooded slopes. The range, half-English with its rolling downs, is in southern India near the beginning of the rugged mountains of the Western Ghats. The temperate climate of the Nilgiris has made it a favorite hot-weather retreat and the hill station of Ootacamund (affectionately referred to as *Ooty*) the most popular resort in the country.

The tea plantations are spread out on every slope, valley and plateau at elevations ranging from one hundred to seven thousand feet. Most of the plantations in southern India are subject to two monsoons a year with annual rainfall averaging anywhere from 50 to 275 inches. Unlike the gardens of northern India where there is a period of winter dormancy, the Nilgiri gardens produce tea throughout the year, the two monsoons a determining factor. The *first flush* is from April to May, when about 25 percent of the annual crop is gathered. The *second flush*, plucked from September to December, yields about 40 percent and the vintage teas, picked in December and January, comprise the rest. Most of the Nilgiri teas are black but some of the green teas have found an appreciative market in Japan. All of the teas are auctioned in Cochin, southern India's only tea auction port.

TEA IN CEYLON

Southeast of the southern tip of India is the small, pear-shape island of Ceylon, known officially as Sri Lanka since 1972. During the late eighteenth century it was called the *Spice Island* and supplied the entire world's need for cinnamon. In the first half of the nineteenth century, Ceylon was introduced to the coffee bean by the British, who had made the island a crown colony. Land was cheap, anyone who wished to could plant the bean and, for the next fifty years, coffee was the island's major agricultural export.

Rosita. A well-known tea factory in Sri Lanka. *Embassy of Sri Lanka, Washington, D.C.*

Coffee plantations increased in total acreage from forty-nine acres in 1834 to thirty-seven thousand in 1845.

In 1869 planters began to notice yellowy-orange blotches on the undersides of the coffee leaves. At first the problem was limited to one district, but within five years, the tiny organism, *Hemileia vastarix* (or, Coffee Rust) had hit every district. At times it appeared as if the fungus disease had been checked, but then it would spring up again, devastate another area, until finally the dead coffee trees were cut up and turned into legs for tea tables.

The planters, most of them hard-working and determined Scotsmen, tried salvaging their land investments by trying other crops. One of them was cinchona, a tree whose bark yields quinine. Encouraged by the British government, they turned to the cinchona as their salvation, invested in seedlings, saw quinine fetch high prices on the London market, increased production, glutted the market and watched prices drop until it became worthless to continue with cinchona.

Three years before the coffee disease struck Ceylon, James Taylor, Scotsman and manager of the many-acre Loolecondera Estate, began planting tea bushes along its paths. His initial investment was in China-type seeds, but the next year he imported two hundred pounds of Assam seed and cleared twenty acres for their growth. His interest in tea had been initiated by Dr. G. H. L. Thwaites, superintendent of the famous Botanical Gardens at Peradeniya. He had experimented with tea planting at the gardens.

But Taylor's plantings were not experimental. They were the first commercial tea plantings on the island. By 1875, Taylor's tea cultivation covered

100 acres; by 1897, the Loolecondera Estate's 1,014 acres held only tea. As more and more planters turned to tea after cinchona, the same pattern followed. Total tea acreage in 1875 was 1,080; 102,000 in 1885; and 305,000 in 1895. Today tea provides Sri Lanka with nearly 70 percent of its export venue from a little less than 600,000 acres under cultivation.

All Ceylon teas are divided into three main categories according to the elevation at which they grow. Generally speaking, "low green" teas—produced below two thousand feet—are characterized by black leaf and colory liquor. Not noted for their flavor, they usually are used to form blends. "Mid-country" teas, grown between two thousand and four thousand feet, have full, rich liquors and a mellow, aromatic flavor. "High grown" teas, cultivated above four thousand feet, often have bright liquors and a particularly excellent flavor. Because of the cooler temperatures they experience, growth is slower than lower down on the estates, and the quality is enhanced.

Within these basic categories, teas from the individual districts possess their own characteristics and the quality can vary with the weather. The finest teas come from the Uva, Maturata and Haputale districts on the eastern slopes of the central mountain range. They are produced in August and September when the southwest monsoon brings heavy rain in the southwest district, while the eastern slopes are normally dry. Uva teas, grown between four thousand and six thousand feet, have a liquor stronger and more distinct from other Ceylon teas and are used widely in the better blends.

Tea estate. *Embassy of Sri Lanka, Washington, D.C.*

Tea pluckers. *Embassy of Sri Lanka, Washington, D.C.*

Teas from the western side of the central mountains—in the districts of Dimbula, Dickoya, Maskeliya and Nuwara Eliya—are best in January and February when that side is dry. Of this group, the most outstanding are the Nuwara Eliya teas, cultivated above six thousand feet and, because of their light liquor, are called the champagne of Ceylon teas. (The distinct quality in all of the teas disappears when the monsoon hits their area.) Because there really is no cold season in Sri Lanka, plucking can go on year round, new shoots growing from the bushes within seven to fourteen days. Most of the five hundred million pounds of annually grown Ceylon tea is sold at auction in Colombo, the balance in London.

*James James
Morrison's Mother
Said to herself, said she:*
*"I can get right down to the end of the town and be back in time for
tea."*

A. A. MILNE, "Disobedience"

Could disease ever attack the tea plant? The possibility that it could served as the catalyst for the founding of the Ceylon Tea Research Institute (T.R.I.) more than fifty years ago. It is headquartered at the St. Coombs Estate four thousand feet up in the green hills of Dimbula.

At one time it did look as if a fungus disease called Blister Blight would be a serious threat to the tea plant, but scientific research at T.R.I. conquered the problem through spraying and pruning. Not all of the Institute's time is devoted to scientific defeat of threatening organisms. One of its major successes has been the development of tea bushes which yield larger crops of higher quality tea, augmented by T.R.I. research in soil improvement, testing of new cultivation methods, and its development of new machinery for manufacturing.

TEA AND INDONESIA

"By fits and starts" is the best way to describe Indonesia's early entry into tea cultivation. At one point, the board of directors of the Dutch East India Company were totally enthused about planting the China seed on Java and importing China labor to tend it. Having proposed the idea in 1728 to a Dutch government reluctantly willing to approve it, the Company dropped the idea the moment it was once again in command of Europe's tea trade.

A century later the idea surfaced anew when a number of China tea seeds were sown successfully in the Buitenzorg Botanical Garden and in an experimental garden outside Garoet. The year was 1827 and the tea did well, but then no one could be found in Java who knew how to prepare it once the two leaves and bud had been plucked.

Java's tea industry credits a Dutch tea taster with getting the fledgling industry into motion. J. I. L. L. Jacobson (were he to sign his name in full, it would run off the page) was en route to China on business when he stopped at Java. The island's commissioner general explained the predicament and prevailed upon Jacobson to go to China on Java's behalf and find out all he could about cultivating and manufacturing the plant a la Chinese. For the next six years he did just that, returning annually to Java with more seeds and more information. On his fifth trip to China, he returned to Java with 300,000 seeds (only 150 were brought back the time before) and twelve Chinese laborers. When the latter were all killed within the year, he made another trip, returning with 7 million seeds and fifteen men (from estate managers to packers). China, not amused at all by Jacobson's wholesale exporting, put a price on his head which immediately made him an island hero. For fifteen years the champion of tea toiled on its behalf, even writing two handbooks on the subject. The first, published in Batavia in 1843, covered cultivation and manufacturing; the second, packing and sorting.

In spite of Jacobson's hard work, the fledgling industry seemed rooted in bad luck, most of its stemming from poor judgment issued by both the government and the East India Company. Land selected for planting was poor, drainage haphazard, plant disease prevalent; though the government owned all the land, controlling agricultural production, it lacked a green thumb with tea which needed careful attention and got very little; transport from gardens to market was unbearably slow over almost impassable roads; and government contracts issued to private tea growers was based on quantity rather than quality of production.

Tired of its unrewarding responsibility, the government withdrew from tea cultivation in the 1860s, turned it over to private ownership and concentrated on the burgeoning coffee industry. The few tea planters now had to battle for survival against a competitor who received the better grade of land for cultivation. The competitive shadows loomed even darker in 1877 when the first Java teas were sent to London auction and received a devastatingly low rating. In short, the tea was badly made and all but unsaleable. Even the lowest grade of India tea was better than Java's best.

A year later, the first seeds from Assam were planted in Java soil and the manufacturing procedures changed to those of India and Ceylon. The next decade saw the gradual elimination of the China jat, introduction of modern equipment and mechanical driers replacing the charcoal furnaces. Plantings expanded and Java's tea, thoroughly improved, became as important as its coffee in world trade.

TEA AND KENYA

East Africa's first tea was planted in 1900 in the botanical gardens at Entebbe, Uganda, where it still flourishes. Three years later, the first plant in Kenya was placed at Limuru, near Nairobi. Of the seven African nations cultivating the plant, Kenya produces triple its nearest rival (Uganda) and, though it took nearly twenty years to gain commercial momentum, tea is—next to coffee—Kenya's most important cash crop.

The principal tea gardens are located on both sides of the Great Rift Valley, part of the geological fault system which cuts across southern Syria, the Dead Sea, the Gulf of Aqaba, the Indian Ocean, and the African continent to Mozambique three thousand miles away. At elevations ranging from five thousand to nine thousand feet, the tea is sown in red earth, a mixture of decomposed rock and volcanic deposits. The tea industry—comprised of small-scale tea holders—operates under the aegis of the ministry of agriculture while the tea board of Kenya exercises licensing control over planting and manufacturing and is empowered to regulate methods of planting, cultivation and processing.

A little over ten years ago, Kenya teas were categorized as "plain teas," used mostly by the trade as inexpensive fillers for blending. Since then, Kenya Tea Development Authority (established in 1964) has worked to improve the tea yields and the quality in the gardens. Next to India tea, Great Britain's largest import is that from Kenya.

7

Tea and the Clipper Ships

WHILE JOHN COMPANY luxuriated in its monopoly of China trade, it easily could afford to send home its cargoes of silks, tea, porcelain, sugar and rhubarb root on ships not noted for speed. There was no competition pressing hard on the stern of its "tea waggons" (an apt sobriquet for the East Indiamen), bent on reaching port and market first. The Company's charter did not call for speed in transit, only that it was "to send orders for tea from time to time, provide ships for its transportation, and always to keep at least one year's supply in their warehouses."

The split in the closed seam came with the long-promised revocation of the Company's Indian monopoly in 1833. It was only a matter of time before the empire's grip on world trade would be challenged. The genesis of the commercial rivalry that would dominate the high seas in the nineteenth century was in the opening of the Erie Canal in 1825—a man-made ribbon of water 360 miles long which took seven years to build. The canal linked the Atlantic coast of New York with the Great Lakes inland. The catalyst for others entering tea trading was the migration westward that followed. With greater access to the West available at cheaper transportation cost, the country opened up and, as it did, so did the market for trade.

The commercial possibilities were not lost upon the merchants who descended on shipbuilders from Baltimore to New England with orders to build the fastest ships they could. Trade with China—particularly in tea—had definite appeal, British monopoly or not. One of the first ships to meet the demand was the *Ann McKim*, built to the specifications of a Baltimore merchant who wanted to improve upon the lines of the Baltimore clippers.

(They, in turn, were an outgrowth of the privateers that roamed the seas during the War of 1812.) Unlike either the privateers or Baltimore clippers, the new era of ships born with the launching of the *Ann McKim* carried three masts and, therefore, more sail.

Named after Isaac McKim's wife, the *Ann McKim* slid into water for the first time on June 4, 1833, the same year in which John Company's singular role in Chinese trade was coming to an end. An account of *Ann McKim's* "debut" appeared in print the following day and can only be viewed as a glowing tribute:

"The launch of the elegant ship *Ann McKim* took place yesterday afternoon in the presence of thousands of spectators. Soon after five o'clock, and at the precise moment that the steamboat *Columbus* was passing the front of the shipyard, she was released from the last stay that prevented her motion, and glided into her destined element in the most beautiful and imposing style amidst the shouts of the assembled multitude. She is a splendid vessel, and richly merits all the praise that has been so universally bestowed on her."

Another newspaper account hailed her as "the most masterly and beautiful specimen of naval architecture which has perhaps ever been produced at the shipyards of this or any other city in the United States."

She was beautiful. One hundred forty-three feet long, thirty-one feet wide, the *Ann McKim* was fitted with the most costly Spanish mahogany combings, rails, and skylights on her flush deck; twelve brass guns; brass bells and brass capstan heads. Sailing the China seas and returning home with chests of tea among her Oriental treasures, she outdistanced every ship. Her beauty and speed, however, far outshone her carrying capacity for both cargo and crew, and Isaac McKim's merchant peers were not overly impressed. But two young naval architects were.

---

*When the tea is brought at five o'clock
And all the neat curtains are drawn with care,
The little black cat with bright green eyes
Is suddenly purring there.*

HAROLD MONRO (1879–1932), "Milk for the Cat"

Donald McKay and John Willis Griffiths first saw the *Ann McKim* when she was berthed in New York for repairs and they were working nearby. The excitement they felt on seeing her stayed with them and, in a few years, was translated on their respective drawing boards into the first of the true clipper ships. Griffiths' *Rainbow* revolutionized marine design. Instead of a full, wide bow that gave way gradually into a narrow stern, the *Rainbow's* widest point was midship, her stern almost as narrow as her bow. She also carried a mass of canvas that was raised higher than any other ship.

The *Rainbow* was launched in New York in 1845 amid cynical bets that she would tip over immediately. She did not. Instead, she almost flew to China and back. On her second trip, which took ninety-two days out and eighty-eight back, she beat the one-way record. Unfortunately, her sea life was short. A storm claimed her on the fifth voyage but not before an even better designed clipper was off Griffiths' drafting table. In 1846, the larger and heavier *Sea Witch* slipped into the waters and into the record books as the fastest vessel then sailing the seven seas. It was a position she held for three years.

When, in 1784, America first entered into trade with China, Britain was not worried about the newcomer's presence. The Company's monopoly was in force, and financial security was guaranteed. And when China refused to renew her contract with John Company (it ended officially in April 1834), opening up Canton to further foreign trade, Britain found solace in numbers. Ships flying the Union Jack far outnumbered those from America or any other country, for that matter, as they sailed up the Pearl River to Whampoa, a muddy village on a barren stretch of island twelve miles south of Canton. There the ships dropped anchor and the cargoes were loaded onto *chop boats* (lighters) for the final haul to Canton and the warehouses at the dock.

British smugness began to change after the Opium War (1840–1842), also known as the Anglo-Chinese War, and the signing of the Treaty of Nanking. There was no question that England had won, but, having done so, she paved the way for foreign encroachment, as well as her own, *into* China. Under the treaty, five more ports were to be made available to foreign residence and trade: Foochow, Shanghai, Canton, Amoy and Ningpo. Hong Kong was to be ceded to Great Britain forever. In all the other articles of the treaty, not one referred to the underlying cause of the war: opium.

Had it not been for England's annual call for greater quantities of tea (nearly thirty million pounds a year by 1830), China might never have been subdued by the opiate which was grown in India under British cultivation, initially by John Company, for express sale in China. This is not to say that China was ignorant of opium before the English came. For centuries opium had been used there as a medicine. Then the Dutch mixed it with tobacco and smoked it to cure intestinal problems; they brought the habit with them to Formosa and from there it came to China. The Chinese, however, chose to smoke opium minus tobacco. Their habit caught on, addiction spread and demand for opium jumped from about two hundred chests (twenty thousand pounds) in the early 1700s to ninety-seven hundred chests in 1830. Ten years later it was double that amount.

Opium was the one item by which British merchants found they could balance the trade in tea. Though much of the tea was paid for in silver, coins and English goods, the Chinese need for British-made merchandise fell far short of the English thirst for tea. The merchants didn't want to pay for the tea only in coin and silver, which the Chinese preferred. After all, what market was there in China for all the bolts of woolens and tweeds when her own brocades and silks were far superior? And what earthly use could be had from countless Birmingham clocks whose faces only the English could read? With opium to trade for tea, trade could be equalized, and the clocks, woolens and tweeds still could be sold.

Opium had been declared illegal by the Ch'ing (Manchu) government in 1729, and, in time, John Company declared trafficking in opium illegal too. But that did not stop private merchants. The Ch'ing government begged England to keep opium away from its shores and sent a trusted official to Canton to oversee the issue and to take whatever measures he thought vital. China no more wished to lose her profitable market in tea than England wished to lose their access to it. But neither did the private traders relish forfeiting their huge successes with opium.

---

*Hail, Drink of Life! how justly shou'd our Lyres
Resound the Praises which thy Pow'r inspires!
Thy Charms alone can equal Thoughts infuse:
Be thou my Theme, my Nectar, and my Muse.*

*Tea, Heav'ns Delight, and Nature's truest Wealth,
That pleasing Physic, and sure Pledge of Health:
The Statesman's Councellor, the Virgin's Love,
The Muse's Nectar, and the Drink of Jove.*

PETER ANTHONY MOTTEUX (1660–1718), *A Poem upon Tea*

Lin Tse-hsu cautioned the English that if they persisted, Canton would be closed to them; he wrote a passionate, if overly dramatic, letter to Queen Victoria in which he apprised her of the poison permeating his land at the pleasure of her subjects, warned of the consequences and threatened customs officials with dire consequences (i.e., execution) if they did not confiscate every ounce of opium within three days' time. (She never received the letter but it did appear in the London *Times*.)

British merchants finally paid heed, took Commissioner Lin at his word and backed off a little. But when an English sailor was killed in a fight, England jumped on the incident, claiming they had jurisdiction of their men in port. It was the flimsiest of excuses on which to base armed conflict, but that is how the war was initiated. Unable to stand up for long against the modern warfare hurled at her, China was forced to the floor by British demands. The ruinous opium seeped further into Chinese life and Britain had her precious tea.

As America continued to encroach upon England's commercial territory in the Orient, the British began to take notice of her growing importance. And when the Navigation Act was repealed, allowing goods to be imported into England on foreign ships, she was compelled to take further note of the faster American clippers and design some of her own. American ships were beating hers home with the new shipments of tea. Competition began in earnest.

Clipper ship. *Peabody Museum of Salem, Massachusetts.*

In 1850, the American ship *Oriental*, only ninety-seven days out of Canton, dropped anchor in London. On board were 1,118 tons of tea. The amount of tea did not make an impression. Her record time did. News of her speed, spread across the pages of the London *Times*, so stunned the British admiralty that they sought—and secured permission to board the vessel and study her lines and construction. They studied well. A year later, the first of the extreme British tea clippers—the *Stornoway* and the *Chrysalite*—sailed for China. From then on, the rivalry between the two countries raged as much on the naval drawing boards as it did on the water.

America's first extreme tea clipper came from Donald McKay, whose design of the *Stag Hound* advanced his country's maritime reputation around the globe. Weighing 1,534 tons and considered near-perfect by those in shipping, the *Stag Hound* was the largest American ship to date when christened the same year as the *Stornoway*. She was fast, once making the Canton to New York run in eighty-five days, and she had a longer sea life than earlier American clippers. Fire finally claimed her in 1861.

In 1851, McKay's second extreme clipper set sail for the first time and, of all the ships, she came to symbolize the romantic period of the clipper. She was 235 feet overall, smaller than the Boston-built *Metropolis*, which sank upon launching, but bigger than the *Ann McKim*. She sailed from New York for California on her maiden voyage, her angel figurehead clutching an extended trumpet, as if to point the way, and docked eighty-nine days later in San Francisco, breaking all records. Her overjoyed owners celebrated by publishing the log of the trip in gold on silk.

For eight years, the *Flying Cloud* (she was that) traveled between China and California and New York, competing in the annual races that became a part of the clipper tradition. In 1859 she was sold to take her place in the Foochow-London run. The annual race between these two ports was *the* sporting event of London, where bets were high on the outcome and the tea industry clung to the latest news to reach Mincing Lane. Prizes—mostly in money—awaited the winning ship and her captain. The vessel received an additional pound sterling per ton of freight and her captain a percentage of the ship's earnings.

Three events took hold of America and turned her attention away from clipper competition during the mid-1800s. In 1849, gold was discovered at Sutter's Mill in California, and for a time it appeared as if all of America were surging westward to find their Eldorado. Gold fever or not, they needed food, tools and merchandise quickly, and marine architects and merchants concentrated on launching ships that could hold larger amounts of the necessary equipment and get it around Cape Horn to the coast in the shortest time possible.

*Come little cottage girl, you seem
To want my cup of tea;
And will you take a little cream?
Now tell the truth to me!*

BARRY PAIN (1864–1928), "The Poets at Tea, Wordsworth"

The same year that gold was found saw the end of the four-year potato famine that wrecked Ireland. Its main crop was ruined by a blight which left the country in dire poverty, thousands dead, equal numbers ailing and even more craving to get out of their homeland. In six years, Ireland's population dropped by two million, two-thirds of which came to the United States between 1847 and 1854. To meet that demand, larger and faster passenger ships came out of the shipyards.

America's Civil War decimated its merchant marine and, by the time it was in a position to begin rebuilding its sailing fleet, two more chapters closed. In 1869, the Suez Canal was opened, thus providing London with a more direct and shorter route to the Orient, and greater use of steam power signaled the autumn days of the tea clippers.

But before the autumn, there was the summer for England. Between 1859 and 1869, twenty-six tea clippers were designed, built and launched, and of that number, six became celebrated. The *Taeping*, launched in 1863; sister ships *Ariel* and *Sir Lancelot*, 1864; *Thermopylae*, 1868; *Cutty Sark*, 1868; and *Blackadder*, 1870. The first two would compete in the Great Tea Race of 1866; *Sir Lancelot*, her figurehead a knight in armor with visor open and right hand removing a sword from its sheath, came in third during the race of 1868 and first the next year; *Thermopylae*, built to withstand the worst of storms, termed the best all-around clipper in the tea fleet, was second in the 1869 race; *Cutty Sark*, designed specifically to rival *Thermopylae*, lost her rudder, jury rudder and the race in the one competition arranged between the two; and *Blackadder*, the only one of the six built entirely of iron, had a dismal maiden voyage, was disliked by the tea merchants and eventually was overshadowed by the steamers.

A touching tribute to *Thermopylae*'s grace of speed came from the captain of the warship *Charybdis*. Both ships cleared Port Phillips Head together and though the captain set every one of his ship's sails to the wind, *Charybdis* could not match *Thermopylae*'s pace. As the latter pulled farther and farther ahead, *Charybdis*'s captain ran up a message with his signal flags:

> Goodbye. You are too much for us. You are the finest model of a ship I ever saw. It does my heart good to look at you.

THE TEA RACE OF 1866

The race began on May 28, 1866, just below Foochow in the Min River. That is, it started there officially but, in fact, the race began with the arrival of the tea chests on sampans from Foochow. And there are those who would say that the race began even earlier—in the offices of the ships' brokers. A lot of money rode on the race and those ships deemed to have the best chance of winning got the first chests of tea and a head start on

Tea clipper. *Peabody Museum of Salem, Massachusetts.*

loading and weighing anchor. Through shifts working around the clock, the tea was loaded by Chinese dock hands and crammed into every available space, while the crews readied their clippers for the sail. Every piece of equipment was inspected minutely and any found to be frayed or showing signs of stress was replaced.

Weighing the heaviest (852 tons) and carrying the largest cargo of tea (1,230,900 pounds), the favored *Ariel* finished loading first and was the first to set sail, but something happened at the start and she had to drop anchor and wait for the next high tide. The 695-ton *Fiery Cross*, with 854,236 pounds of tea on board, sailed past her and gained a day's lead, followed by *Serica* (708 tons and 954,236 pounds of tea) and *Taeping* (767 tons and 1,108,709 pounds of tea) edging past the Min River bar together. Between May 31 and June 7, the remaining seven ships in the race weighed anchor.

On June 15, the *Fiery Cross* and *Ariel* rounded the Cape of Good Hope within a couple of hours of each other, with *Taeping* twelve hours behind and the remaining ships even further in back. But, as the clippers made their way up the Atlantic coast of the African continent, *Serica, Taeping, Ariel, Fiery Cross* and *Taitsing* (which had started out May 31) were very close to each other. On August 4, *Ariel, Fiery Cross* and *Taeping* crossed the Equator together, *Serica* was two days away and *Taitsing* a week. By August 10, *Ariel* led *Fiery Cross* and on August 17, *Taeping* pulled ahead of the latter, which was becalmed for twenty-four hours.

Though she had lost a full day to the still winds, *Fiery Cross* was right behind *Ariel* and ahead of *Taeping* and *Serica* when they all passed the Western Isles on August 29. *Fiery Cross* was ninety-two days out of Foochow, the other three ninety-one. *Taitsing*, ninety-three days out, passed two days later.

As the ships approached Channel entry, westerly winds sent *Ariel* ahead. In his private log, her Captain Keay wrote: "A ship, since daylight, has been in company on starboard quarter—*Taeping* probably." On shore, observers posted at each headland kept track of the ships' positions and reported them to the nearest post office. The invention of the telephone was still eleven years in the future, so news had to be carried by signal, courier and horseback. Even so, London was kept abreast of the extremely tight race.

The winning of the race was dependent as much upon the sharpness of the captain as it was upon the winds. Captain Keay missed nothing. In his log he noted on September 6, 5:00 a.m.: "Saw the *Taeping* running and also signaling; bore up lest they should run eastward of us and get pilot first; seeing us keep away, they hove to, we again hove to."

A half hour later he recorded: "Saw two cutters coming out of Dungeness Roads." And, ten minutes later: "Kept away so as to get between *Taeping* and the cutters." At 5:55 a.m.: "Rounded to close to the pilot cutter and got first pilot. Were saluted as first ship from China this season. I replied, 'Yes, and what is that to the westward? We have not room to boast yet. Thank God we are first up Channel and hove to for a pilot an hour before him.' "

At 8:00 a.m., *Ariel* sailed through The Downs off the southern coast of England, *Taeping* ten minutes behind her. *Serica* passed through at noon, *Fiery Cross* in the early hours of the next morning and *Taitsing* before noon on September 9.

Unbeknownst to the captains of the *Ariel* and *Taeping*, their anxious owners had entered into a secret pact. Tension (and surely tempers too) was at such high pitch over the tightness of the race—a race which could not be won truly until the first chests of tea literally hit the London wharfs —that the ship owners decided to split the winner's extra earnings of ten shillings per ton.

On September 7, *Taeping*, leeward of *Ariel* and closer to the English shore, spotted the smoke of a tug and set her prow in its direction. She became the first in the race to take in sail and be pulled to Gravesend, "gateway to the Port of London" on the river Thames. *Ariel* was pulled in fifty-five minutes later and, after a wait for the tide, entered the gates of India Dock at 10:23 p.m. *Taeping*, berthing at London Docks, had farther to go up the Thames and reached the Docks entrance at 10:00 p.m. According to her records, she docked twenty minutes ahead of *Ariel* and was the first to have her tea hurled over the side. *Serica*, which had won the previous year from *Fiery Cross*, pulled into West India Dock at 11:30 p.m., just before the gates were to close. In all, the three clippers had taken 102 days to sail three-quarters around the globe.

THE LEADMAN'S SONG
(author unknown)

For England, when with favoring gale,
Our Gallant ship up Channel steered,
And scudding, under easy sail,
The high blue wester lands appeared,
To heave the lead the seaman sprang,
And to the pilot cheerly sang,
   "By the deep—Nine."

And bearing up to gain the port,
Some well-known object kept in view,
An abbey tower, a ruined fort,
A beacon to the vessel true;
While oft the lead the seaman flung,
And to the pilot cheerly sung,
   "By the mark—Seven."

And as the much-loved shore we near,
With transport we behold the roof
Where dwelt a friend or partner dear,
Of faith and love and matchless proof.
The lead once more the seaman flung,
And to the watchful pilot sung,
   "Quarter less—Five."

Now to her berth the ship draws nigh,
With slackened sail she feels the tide,
Stand clear the cable is the cry,
The anchor's gone, we safely ride.
The watch is set, and through the night,
We hear the seaman with delight
Proclaim—"All's well."

8

Customs and Manners, Past and Present

A TRAVELER trekking the more desolate regions of Asia would not be off the mark were he to cram a fair number of tea bags into his knapsack. To be sure, they would make a comforting drink, but they might also come in handy for trade.

Tea in place of money? The idea is not as far-fetched as it might sound. In such circumstances, neither the well-promoted travelers checks nor currency would be of earthly use to nomadic tribes or truly isolated villagers whose paths the traveler might cross. But, should he need some food or equipment or even a passable donkey or horse, he might be able to get them in exchange for the tea from a few bags.

Using tea as money is a custom which originated in China not long after tea acquired its distinct place in Chinese culture. At that time, the value of currency remained at full strength only as long as it circulated within a short distance from where it was first issued. The farther afield the currency was taken, the lesser its value, while tea's value as currency increased beyond the borders of the tea gardens. The idea of tea as money has continued through time to the present and the custom can still be found existing in sections of Tibet and in the southwest portion of China. Tea currency is not carried loose but in the form of compressed bricks, decorated on both sides with scenes of temples or gardens, with animals, with writings or, as in the case of Russian tea money, with regiments of stamps signifying place of origin. If the owner of the brick money were ever thirsty, he merely chipped off to make a drink.

In order to drink tea in the home of a Tibetan, it helps to have a strong stomach and taste buds that do not shock easily. With all due respect to the mountainous kingdom (now absorbed by China) and to its refugees who have carried the tea custom with them into Nepal and across other borders, their tea would never do in fashionable circles—or even in a farmer's kitchen, for that matter.

The first thing offered to a visitor to a monastery, a village or a person's home is their unique yak butter tea. It is consumed before conversation takes place—a feat which can take a while to accomplish. Tibetans love tea, drink huge amounts of it, allow it to steep a long, long time (about an hour) before adding lots of salt and then churning the entire liquid with butter made from yak milk. The concoction takes on a dismal, rancid taste (yaks are not particular about what they eat) and a disquieting appearance —it looks rather oily with the butter fat floating on top. Once churned, the tea (the term is used advisedly) is poured into a teapot and then served to everyone in individual brass cups.

The entire Tibetan family convenes at home when a visitor comes by. (Home is a three-floor mud adobe-style hut with the animals living on the first floor, the family on the second and the third floor—reached by crawling up narrow stairs—is reserved for animal fodder and firewood makings). Tea is taken grouped around the room wherever there is space, on pillows or on the floor, and if the visitor is still there later in the day, then he may have the opportunity to partake of another meal with tea—this time with the addition of heavy wheat cakes.

THE SAFFRON PERIOD IN HOLLAND

A more delicate ambience awaited the guests who called upon the Dutch hostesses during the first half of the eighteenth century. As mentioned in an earlier chapter, the women of Holland were extremely proud of their assortment of teas, the tiny, fragile teacups imported from China and the one room in each of their houses reserved for tea time.

Tea time usually began early in the afternoon—around two or three— when guests would convene in the special room, there to sit down and warm their feet (summer or winter) on foot-stoves. The Dutch hostess followed a ritual not too unlike the formality expressed during the Japanese tea ceremony. An assemblage of porcelain and silver filigree tea boxes, each containing a different tea, were placed next to the hostess. After making certain of her guests' comfort, she asked each one their tea preference and usually the guests deferred to the hostess's selection. With that ritual completed, the hostess filled the small cups and, for those who preferred combining saffron with their tea, she gave a pot of saffron too. The saffron was poured into the cup, sugar was added and stirred and then the tea was poured into the saucer.

In those days, it was judged improper to drink tea from the cup. Needless to say, while the ladies may not have lapped up the tea like a pleased cat with milk, some slurped while others sipped, the audible sounds of delight mixing together and canceling any need for conversation to break the silence. What chitchat ensued zeroed in on the splendid tea and the cakes and sweets accompanying it. After scads of cups—rather, saucers—had been consumed (anywhere from ten to forty each), the delighted ladies repaired to brandy and pipes. Yes, they smoked too.

EARLY ENGLISH CUSTOMS

When the Portuguese princess became the English queen and brought tea to her husband's court, tea became a part of London's culture. But it was so expensive that it was taken in small amounts, the cups little larger than an ample thimble. During the next century, its price fell, but not far enough to turn it into a household commodity. To make certain that their servants didn't try to sneak some, mistresses kept their tea caddies under lock and key in plain view in the living room. The caddies—often made in pairs to hold different teas—were fashioned of tortoiseshell, silver or brass.

The English were not without their own peculiarities when it came to socializing over tea. Once a cup was empty, ladies either placed their spoon across its top, turned the cup into the saucer or used the spoon to tap the cup and summon husband or escort to remove it. Scottish women stayed with their cup until everyone else's was empty before having it refilled. To ensure that each received back her original cup, it became customary for spoons to carry numbers. And, speaking of spoons, the Scots also had the odd habit of standing their spoon straight in the cup after stirring in the sugar. It must have done wonders for the face.

By the end of the eighteenth century, the high price of tea could not keep the rest of England from drinking it. It became the principal beverage for all classes, as noted by the Comte de la Rochefoucauld in 1784. Touring England, he wrote: "Throughout the whole of England the drinking of tea is general. You have it twice a day and though the expense is considerable, the humblest peasant has his tea just like the rich man." Thirteen years later, Sir Frederick Eden echoed tea's widespread use: "Any person who will give himself the trouble of stepping into the cottages of Middlesex and Surrey at meal times, will find that in poor families tea is not only the most usual beverage in the morning and evening, but is generally drunk in large quantities after dinner."

Credit for originating afternoon tea—that delicious hour so treasured by every English person and Anglophile—is given to Anna, Duchess of Bedford (1788–1861). As the eighteenth century ceded to the nineteenth, the gap between breakfast and dinner—the two main meals of the day—

expanded considerably. One or one-thirty lunch, at which servants were not in attendance and everyone fended for the self, tended to be more of a postscript to breakfast than a preface to eight o'clock dinner. The widening gap without consumption of food proved discomforting to the Duchess who, tiring of her fainting spells, switched the habit of after-dinner tea to before-dinner tea.

At first (around 1840), she took afternoon tea in the secrecy of her boudoir, gradually inviting in a few friends to join her in "containing the pangs of hunger." The idea was captivating and soon the novel social event was copied widely. By mid-century, afternoon tea was out of the boudoir and into the living room. The simple bread and butter first served with the tea was soon augmented by a range of foodstuffs.

Wafer-thin sandwiches minus crusts and filled with egg, tomato, cucumber, chicken, jam, shrimp or fish pâté shared the tea table with hot buttered scones, crumpets and toasted breads kept warm on a silver-plated dish supported over a water jacket filled with hot water. *Patum Pepperium*, a highly flavored paste spread on hot buttered toast, guaranteed thirst but was highly popular. Following the sandwiches, another cup of tea would be taken with a light sponge cake filled with fresh cream or jam; iced cakes garnished with nuts, fruit or coconut shreds; slab fruit cakes; and French pastries.

The first pot of tea was usually prepared in the kitchen and brought into the living room in a silver pot or one of fine china which matched the cups, saucers and plates. The second pouring was most often done by the hostess with the addition of hot water held in a silver-plated kettle heated underneath by a spirit lamp. A quilted tea cozy, made of silk or velvet, kept the teapot warm. The tea hour usually began at 4:00 or 4:30 and lasted just that—an hour.

First period bone china teapot with parapet and gold line decoration. C. 1815. *Josiah Wedgwood & Sons, Ltd.*

Afternoon tea need not be a formal affair and it can be taken outdoors as easily as in. Informal gatherings of friends might find tea being served in the library or solarium or even around the dining table with a modest tea service at hand. In more plain circumstances, brown earthenware or stoneware teapots replaced those in silver. Outdoor English teas contained the flavor of picnics and a bucolic atmosphere. Tea was served on the terrace, guests taking time off from playing croquet or tennis, or from strolling about the grounds. The garden teas for which the English are so famous were held usually on weekends and attended by both men and women.

In the more industrial and rural areas of Britain, dinner was taken midday, followed around 6:00 by another meal known as High Tea. A cooked dish accompanied the usual bread and butter and scones. It might be sausages and mashed potatoes, kippers or fried fish, an egg dish or a cold plate of meat with tomatoes. High tea was practically on the table the moment the men walked in from their jobs in factories, offices or the fields.

TEA MEETINGS

In tea, temperance societies of England found their greatest ally. The movement against alcohol took hold in the 1830s when do-gooders convened in the urban cities where drunkards were in high number and fair prominence (visibly, not socially). Reformed characters were as much in attendance at these meetings as were individuals known more for their grace of beauty, wealth and intelligence.

Observers of the social scene were quick to point out that tea after dinner, instead of port and brandy, returned the English gentleman to his living room and family "in a state of gentlemanly sobriety"—obviously a state not usually prevalent. The morality of tea was not lost upon those who attended the meetings where they saw the reformed drunkards speak of their hard times and new lives, and who sat down at tables for a complete tea. These meetings proved loathsome to the sober Charles Dickens (who found them hypocritical), and he took out his dislike through his writings. In *Pickwick Papers* he writes of a tea meeting at which a young woman was "swellin wisibly" after nine cups of tea.

LATER ENGLISH CUSTOMS

During the latter part of Queen Victoria's reign an extraordinary custom became associated with afternoon tea. For certain gentlemen it assumed an importance quite unintended, a time for flirtation uninterrupted and the possibility of receiving "the ultimate favour."

First period hand-painted bone china tea service decorated by John Cutts. C. 1812–1815. *Josiah Wedgwood & Sons, Ltd.*

How much sexual activity could transpire with a bastion of steel corsets or whalebones and laces to overcome has never been made clear. But the enterprising aristocrats in England and France followed a certain routine, formal at the start and then each to his own devices:

Upon the appointed hour, the gentleman would arrive for tea at the home of his hostess, a member of his social circle whose husband might be sounding the bell at just that moment outside someone else's house. Let in by the butler or footman, the visiting gentleman did not hand over his cane, hat and gloves—and, perhaps, cape—as was the custom on other occasions. Instead he carried them into the living room where he was received and lay them on the floor beside the chair in which he sat. This gesture was supposed to convey the intention that he had just popped in for a moment—as a surprise, no doubt—and would be leaving in the instant.

For whom was this covert gesture intended? For anyone who might accidentally open the living room doors once they were closed. It was an understood fact in England that once living room doors were shut, the servants were not to open them under any circumstances unless summoned by bell. But a suspicious husband or jealous swain could barge in as easily as not. Just what explanation could be given—and be accepted—were that to happen and the hostess found in some state of deshabille is amusing to speculate. "Just popped in for a quick cup" would hardly be convincing enough.

Imagine—in England and in France—it is four o'clock of an afternoon and on countless parquet or marble floors hats, gloves and canes lie still while tea grows cold as an afternoon's conquest is sought. Such charades finally succumbed in the early 1900s to overuse, disbelief and The Great War.

The decline of the Tea Gardens in the middle of the nineteenth century left a social vacuum in which middle-class ladies could take tea with their friends outside their homes. The aristocratic ladies could convene at a number of higher class establishments or at pastry shops where a few tea tables were introduced. But the tea shops that were to make such an impression, especially in London, did not emerge until the last two decades of the nineteenth century. All had their origin from a habit initiated by the woman manager of a branch of the Associated Bread Company (known to all as ABC) in the City of London. She began the trend by inviting one or two friends and favored customers into the back room of her shop for tea. Her suggestion was received with as much enthusiasm as was the Duchess of Bedford's original idea, that the taking of tea was removed to

Queen's Ware
S.Y.P. (Simple
Yet Perfect) tea-
pot. C. 1900.
*Josiah Wedgwood
& Sons, Ltd.*

the front of the shop where tables were set up. The managers of other ABC branches agreed to try out the idea and, before long, tea shops had achieved their own importance in the social life of women. Of all the tea shop chains, perhaps Lyons—with as many as 250 branches around the world—became the most famous. Its origins are said to have stemmed from one Maria Tewk, who lived during the first half of the eighteenth century, ran a tea house without a license (because women were not allowed to be given licenses), was fined time and again before she was finally granted a license and subsequently founded the forerunner of the Lyons shops.

Tea was not denied the traveler be he (or she) aboard ship, train or plane. Ocean liners broke the morning with soup at eleven and tea at four, although it was available at any hour of the day or night too. Early flights took along flasks of tea and hot water to be served at the proper hour, while train terminals dispensed tea from tea rooms and from tea trolleys rolled across the platforms. The tea trolleys were especially busy when trains stopped at stations in the middle of the night to discharge some passengers and give others a chance to buy a cup's worth. Train passengers with sleeping-berth compartments could have tea made for them at any hour by the car attendant or could take High Tea in the restaurant car, while those who preferred remaining in their compartments the entire time could make use of the tea basket. Available at stations any hour of the day, the baskets held the full makings for tea plus several slices of buttered bread, some cake, and fruit. When finished consuming its contents, the traveler shoved the basket under the train seat from which it was retrieved at journey's end and returned to the station of origin.

An established custom begun in the 1920s was the morning break for tea in offices, ministries and factories. A refreshing break, it contributed to increased work activity and became as much a part of office procedure as the afternoon break for tea.

In recent years, the fresh-made tea served in offices by the "tea lady" from her tea trolley—fashioned after those at the stations—has been replaced by vending machines and left workers with the nagging taste that they have been short-changed in favor of immediacy. While a "cuppa" is ready at the instant with a push of a button and a drop of a coin, the quality of the drink can hardly compare with that made by the venerable tea ladies of the past.

More than one tea tradition has disappeared since the Second World War. Custom service on trains is all but a memory. Garden tea parties—to which the men wore top hats and grays and the women wide-brimmed hats and summer prints—are a rarity, as are the quaint tea rooms of the suburbs and the habit of private home owners in the country acknowledging—through the display of a sign bearing the word TEA—that tea is served of an afternoon for a small sum.

Afternoon tea can still be taken in both city and suburban hotels. Bread and butter or sandwiches, toasted something and a cake or two comprise the tea menu. Of the London hotels, Claridges provides perfect service with elegant bone china; the Palm Court of the Ritz, popular with Americans, has a fresh linen-and-flowers ambience; Browns has delicious food, elegant service and a very cozy home atmosphere; and The Dorchester has perhaps the most expensive but perfect afternoon tea.

AMERICAN TEA TRIVIA

After the various American tea parties set England on its ear and the colonists to war, peace returned to the New World and tea was no longer banished from the tables. Americans had been quite serious about their involvement with tea. Furniture designed specifically for tea filled many a home—tea tables, stands for the kettles, tray-topped tables, all made from expensive woods; elaborate teapots of silver and brass and earthenware, and the finest cups, saucers and sandwich plates of beautifully painted china. Allowing them to remain unused for four years was a measure of strength England never imagined possible.

The oldest and largest teapot of its kind in the world, 1875. Vital statistics: age—100 years old in 1975; height—37 inches; width—38½ inches; depth—28 inches; weight (empty)—69 lbs.; weight (filled)—492 lbs.; capacity—38 gallons, enough to serve 972 cups of tea. *Used with permission of the Kellogg Company.*

Though coffee had replaced tea during the revolution, it continued to hold prominence mainly at breakfast. The early evening meal in America still was fashioned around tea. That came to an end the last decade of the nineteenth century when the midday meal lost its importance to the evening meal of dinner, and coffee, served at the earlier meal, became a part of the evening one.

Afternoon tea continued to be served in the aristocratic homes of New York, Boston, Philadelphia and Wilmington. But its real American resurgence came with the craze for daytime dancing. A phenomenon of sorts, daytime dancing rose to its frenzy during the period 1910–mid-twenties. Tea was served and tea dancing acquired its name. Tea dancing produced a variety of reactions—not all of them pleasant. The Maxie, Turkey Trot and Bunny Hug were the rage, the one-step Turkey Trot considered so immoral that the *Ladies' Home Journal* fired fifteen of its employees—all women—for doing it on their lunch break. A Broadway producer vowed to fire any members of his chorus caught doing the T.T. Why was it such a no-no? Because the partners danced close to each other. Before long, however, the T.T. was out of favor and the Castle Walk, Shimmy and several versions of the tango were in. In the 1919 Ziegfeld Follies, star Bert Williams shook the audience with his counter to Prohibition, complaining that "You Can't Make Your Shimmy Shake on Tea."

The better hotels in cities big and small still serve afternoon tea upon request. During the "war" on high coffee prices in the mid-1970s, a number of first-class hotels revived the afternoon tea habit, but the pace of the cities never allowed it to become a favored vogue. Among the New York hotels that do serve afternoon tea are the Plaza in its Palm Court, the Algonquin (rendezvous of the literary), the Sherry-Netherland and the Drake. The legendary Russian Tea Room in New York serves tea all day and far into the night, with afternoon tea and pastries—if such an hour can be slotted in their all-day servings—between 3:30 and 4:30. Only Russian tea is poured at any time.

Soda fountains and diners will serve up a cup of tea or iced tea as easily as they will a chocolate sundae or greasy hamburger. The tea is made from a tea bag and quite often the bag is not even in the cup, which is filled with hot water, but resting on the saucer.

RUSSIA

The tea that first came to Russia across the overland route through Manchuria and Mongolia came in solid bricks. The Russian tea is really tea from China, sometimes a blend of mainland and Taiwan leafs. Russian aristocracy developed a highly distinctive tea-drinking style. A samovar, a large water-heating urn made of silver, brass or copper, is the focal point. A teapot of strong tea rests on its top, the concentrate poured into glasses with silver holders and diluted with the hot water from the samovar. Milk is not taken with Russian tea, a slice of lemon is. Some Russians prefer to add jam to their tea in place of lemon; others sweeten the taste by placing a lump of sugar between the teeth and sipping the tea. The Russians are enamored of tea and consume it throughout the day.

MOROCCO

In the wealthier Moroccan homes, a tea maker is not considered unusual. Tea-drinking only dates back in Morocco to 1854 when the British, their ships blocked from the Baltic, sought new markets for their goods and managed to dispose of considerable chests of tea in Morocco. Latecomers though they may be to tea, Moroccans have adopted it as their daily and universal drink.

Tea-making in Morocco is without rules and no two glasses ever taste quite the same. Pots of brass or silver are used—china and earthenware ones are a thing of the past. After the meal is finished and the table cleared away, the tea maker comes in first with a tray bearing pastries veiled in muslin, a carved box holding tea and sugar, and a bowl of mint which she places at the host's side. Incense impregnates the air, and rose water in embossed silver bottles is passed around to refresh face, neck and hands of the guests.

> *The cozy fire is bright and gay,*
> *The merry kettle boils away*
> *And hums a cheerful song.*
> *I sing the saucer and the cup;*
> *Pray, Mary, fill the teapot up,*
> *And do not make it strong.*
>
> BARRY PAIN, "The Poets at Tea, Cowper"

The tea maker returns with a silver tray filled with colored glasses and offers to each guest before bringing in the smoking samovar. The tea is always green, the leaves coarse or fine, scented or not, sometimes containing opium, and infused either alone or with sprigs of mint. True tea connoisseurs in Morocco never add mint to the first pot of tea. The only mint allowed to be used with tea is the "Mentha viridis," the best quality dark and with firm stalks. (The working Moroccan on his way home buys his few sprigs of mint from a street seller squatted behind a "bushful" he has decorated with an occasional rose.) When mint is hard to find during the winter months, sage or wormwood is often substituted. Basil, marjoram and peppermint are used occasionally, while an infusion of amber is both rare and refined. In summertime, orange blossoms sometimes accompany the mint.

At formal receptions, two teapots are used, not as one might suspect, one at a time, but together. The host—or the tea maker—stands or sits with a pot held high in each hand. The liquid from each is then poured at the same time into the same glass. A certain dexterity is in order if the pourer is not to soak either himself or his nearest guests. Sugar is never added to the individual glasses, only to the pots. And if a guest takes one cup of tea, Moroccan etiquette requires that he take three.

IRAN

Not a waking hour passes that an Iranian misses a cup of tea without good reason. It is the country's national drink, although the only meal at which it is served is breakfast (with bread and cheese). Scented tea is a favorite of Iranians, who will add blossoms or herbs to their canisters and leave them closed for several days.

The drink is so much a part of Iran's social manners that it is even offered to one's enemy. If served (to friend or foe) in the home, the eldest woman living there does the honors, seated on a rug made especially for the ritual. A small amount of tea is placed in a glass held by a silver "estekan," water is taken from the samovar, sugar and lemon are added afterward. The tea is then poured into saucers, a sugar cube is dipped into it and put under the tongue to melt, and the tea is sipped from the saucer.

In the traditional Persian tea houses, the *chi-khaneh*, benches filled with cushions line the edges of the room. Low tables are used in the Hilton Hotel's *chi-khaneh* in Tehran. The samovar, heated either with coal or kerosene, is *always* going, and a filled saucer is visible somewhere in the room.

*Matrons, who toss the cup, and see
The grounds of fate in grounds of tea.*

ALEXANDER POPE (1688–1744), *An Essay on Man*

Tea houses in Iran are normally segregated by a screen in the small villages, men on one side, women on the other, while the Family Tea houses obviously welcome both sexes together. Music is a part of the ambience of a tea house, traditional or religious music played by an *ashik* on his instrument as he sings along. The *mullah*—or religious leader—is often to be found in tea houses talking to his students or someone studying the Koran.

The most historic of Iran's tea houses are the caravansaries, built during the fifteenth century and stretching from one border to the other. An exaggerated extension of the tea house, they were built around a rectangular court with cubicles sheltering the camel traveler. Once a major tourist attraction, Ab Ambar in Tehran is a tea house with a water cellar and collection of art around it, sitting on pillars and built during the Qujar dynasty (A.D. 700–1199).

AUSTRALIA

While coffee continues to rise in popularity, tea-drinking is the most consistent pastime in Australia. The mid-morning and the mid-afternoon rest periods in private and government offices are still known as "tea breaks." In factories they tend to be called "smokoh's."

Water is boiled by electric jug or kettle and poured over the tea leaves in a teapot made of earthenware, metal or heat resistant glass. Rule of thumb—inherited from the Mother Country—is "one teaspoon per person and one for the pot." Tea bags are slowly gaining acceptance in Australia, used mostly when one cup of tea is being made. The bag is either "dunked" or "jiggled" in the boiling water.

In the real outback of Australia, whether men are working or people are camping out, the *billy* is their dearest possession. A tin can of varying sizes, the *billy* is used to boil water. Its fairly solid swinging wire handle is used to hold the can and to hook on a fork of wood over the flames until the water boils. Tea is added when the water comes to a boil and, because outbackers like their tea strong, it can be left to boil until it is one very dark, tannin-tasting drink.

Some outbackers take the billy's handle and swing the near-boiling container in a vertical circle to "settle the leaves" at the billy's bottom. Others content themselves with putting the billy on the ground and tapping its side with a spoon. The end result is the same but there is a greater flair of adventure—or dramatics—in the former.

When the outbacker, also known as a *swaggie* or *swagman*, rises in the morning, the billy is the first thing for which he reaches and usually the last thing he puts down at night. Between those two gestures, the billy remains simmering over the fire until it is time for the next cup—rather, the next billy of tea. And when it is time for the swagman to move on, he wraps his tea, tea utensils and billy in his swag—called by every outbacker his *Matilda*—and goes on his way. How the cloth swag got that name, no one knows. But, Matilda it is, celebrated in a song synonymous with Australians and sung with great feeling wherever her troops have traveled. The name of the song is "Waltzing Matilda," and it carries the lilting refrain, "And he sang as he watch'd and waited till his billy boil'd 'You'll come a-waltzing Matilda with me.'"

TAIWAN

On the island of Taiwan, the Chinese favor green tea and call black tea *red* because of the color it imparts to the water. Some families drink tea only when receiving guests, considering it a gesture of respect not to be diluted with common use. On formal occasions, tea is served in delicate cups; other times, in glasses with a top to put on them between sips to retain its warmth. While many of the young have become more Westernized in their habits and drink lots of iced tea (when they aren't guzzling Cokes), some of the elders will take only tea, never plain water.

SRI LANKA

In the remote villages of Sri Lanka (Ceylon) a cluster of bananas dangling above or beside a shop door identifies it as a Tea Boutique. It is to these Tea Boutiques that villagers will come after a day's work in the tea gardens and take a cup of tea, chew on a betel leaf and chat with friends.

The tea water is boiled in an urn similar to a samovar, fueled by coconut shell charcoal. A cloth strainer holds a large amount of tea over which the boiled water is poured. It takes a while for the water to trickle through the leaves and into a brass cup. Once the cup is filled, the hot tea is poured from one brass cup to another until it has cooled.

Although considered veritable newcomers to tea, Sri Lankans look upon the drink with as much veneration as the Japanese, even if they eliminate the ceremony. (Remember, tea saved their economy.) In city homes, tea is prepared the English way—served with milk and sugar—consumed any hour of the day and drunk from fine china. Afternoon tea in Sri Lanka is accompanied by *agtalla*, a mixture of rice and sugar seasoned with pepper and salt and rolled into a ball. Cookies or pastries of the host country accompany tea offered at Sri Lankan embassies. Other than at breakfast, tea is never taken with meals, only between them and, for many, as a soothing nightcap. Iced tea is still having a hard time catching on among Sri Lankans. Even in the hottest and most humid periods, hot tea cools its drinker.

JAPAN

In daily life, the Japanese serve hot tea throughout their meals, cup after cup drunk from handleless receptacles. Green tea, or *o-cha*, is the Japanese favorite and is to them what coffee is to Americans. Neither milk nor sugar is added, although the Japanese will add lemon to the black tea, *ko-cha*, taken when dining on Western cuisine. The flavor of green tea is so well liked that it turns up in ice cream, candy and a liqueur. It also is found in *chazuke*, a very Japanese food which combines both the flavor and the aroma of green tea with rice. *Chazuke* is served in the home and though it is among the simplest of meals, some restaurants specialize in it.

Because the Japanese have such an affinity for rating everything—from sake to sumo wrestlers—according to quality, tea is rated too. Green tea is rated according to the different leaves and the processes that go into finishing the teas. *Gyokuro* is the pet of the connoisseur, picked from the best of the old bushes whose carefully tended new buds are shaded from the sun by reed screens.

Of the high quality teas used most by the Japanese, *sencha* is from the best leaves of the regularly cultivated plants while the coarser-leafed *bancha* comes from plants picked at season's end. *Bancha* is usally given to the very young and the very old. *Matcha* is used for the tea ceremony, a finer ground *matcha* for iced tea.

What a part of confidante has that poor teapot played ever since the kindly plant was introduced among us! What myriads of women have cried over it, to be sure! What sick-beds it has smoked by! What fevered lips have received refreshment from it! Nature meant very kindly by women when she made the tea-plant; and with a little thought, what a series of pictures and groups the fancy may conjure up and assemble round the teapot and cup.

WILLIAM MAKEPEACE THACKERAY, *Pendennis*

The Japanese revere tea even today (*o-cha* means "honorable tea") and it is custom, upon arising, for a cup of tea to be offered first at the altar of one's ancestors, then a cup given to one's parents, before taking a cup oneself. Tea houses are prevalent in every city and town, the drink automatically brought the moment one comes in. (This applies too when eating in a restaurant.) Tea is served during business conferences, at diplomatic discussions, and during transactions of any kind, regardless of the hour. Tea can be bought at train stations before boarding time, just as was the habit before the war. The only thing that has changed is the bottle. The bottle containing the tea (enough for two small cups) used to be of green glass. Now it is disposable. So is the cup.

9

Tea in War

IT IS NOT LIKELY that tea's permanence in the life-style of the British will ever be questioned. But it may be harder to accept without doubt that tea has had an extraordinary role in wars, and that quite often, the courage to continue fighting, to take those important extra steps, were frequently abetted and solaced by cups of tea. After the Battle of Waterloo, the Duke of Wellington said: "Tea cleared my head and left me with no misapprehensions."

Tea followed the British troops into France during World War I, cups filled with sugar and condensed milk handed out at odd hours of the day—not necessarily at the customary tea-drinking hour, but then, who could be certain of still being around at four o'clock of that afternoon? The sergeant who really thought of his men—and who received a fair amount of reluctant respect in return—was the one who made certain that everyone had their rations of tea or that the water was ready for the boil.

At war's end, tea's importance in that conflict was profiled in the London *Times*: "The solvent that is tea accommodated a thousand inter-relationships which threatened friction. The submarine sinkings, the convoy system, the munition question, the War Cabinet itself were suspended regularly every afternoon for a few minutes when the little black teapot made its pre-emptory appearance, flanked with what had once been toast and cake, but what were toast and cake no longer. With it returned a certain Georgian virility."

Tea's importance was no less felt during the next world war when, on July 8, 1940, England's Ministry of Foods announced it would be rationed. Two ounces a week per person, purchasable in any of four-week combinations to take advantage of existing retail packet sizes (quarter-, half- and one-pound weights). In deference to individual preferences of brands, the ministry did not put restrictions on where tea could be bought. The English were free to cross city or county lines if need be, instead of being able to go only to neighborhood shops.

During the early days of rationing, tea coupons were a part of the regular coupon book. In the summer of 1942, which produced the fifth edition of ration books, tea was given its own coupon with its name stamped in large letters. With this edition, tea coupons became unavailable for young children. They probably never got any tea to begin with because most of the complaints received by the ministry on this decision came from the elderly—presumably grandparents of the children. Criticism over the act stopped only in 1944 when the minister of foods announced an extra weekly ration for those over seventy.

> *Here thou great Anne! whom three realms obey,*
> *Dost sometimes counsel take—and sometimes tea.*
>
> ALEXANDER POPE, *The Rape of the Lock*, Canto III

After the individual rationing of tea was deemed logical and fair, another problem—rather critical—arose. How could tea be allotted for mid-morning, afternoon and evening cups to those not at home during those periods, but at work or on volunteer civilian duty somewhere? The Red Cross worker, the fire-watcher, the roof-spotter, the coastal observer outside all night? First-aid volunteers, employees in business and government offices, farm hands, civilian defense units marshaled about the countryside? None of them would have access to the mobile canteens that traveled the streets, bringing cups of the blessed drink when needed most (as much for moral support as for warmth).

Office workers brewed their own, the farmer and his help in the fields were brought their afternoon tea from the farmhouse. As for the countless volunteers threading in and out of doors, they could hardly be expected to carry a primus stove, tin cup and teapot or saucepan around as they checked the skies, the roofs, cellars, small fires, etc. To cover that problem, the ministry allocated an extra—albeit small—allowance of tea under warrant of "Office Tea Clubs," with the proviso that at least four hours per day was spent on the job (paid or not) and that the tea was to be used communally. The only ones to lose out on the extra allowance were those who worked alone.

The mobile canteens became a comforting part of the London scene during the Battle of Britain in 1940. After concentrating their bombs on England's coastal defense stations, shipping and radar posts, the Germans switched their devastating attack on the cities as a prelude to their invasion plans. Heavy bombings rained on the cities with brutal nightly onslaughts on London that began September 7 and lasted until the end of October, forcing Londoners to spend their nights in shelters.

The mobile canteens began their work as night fell, snaking through bombed-out and fire-ridden streets to service the shelters on their routes. Even under the most stressing times, the English expect a good "cuppa," and when it does not come forth, they are apt to criticize what did. The gratitude, the thanksgiving felt by so many at the mere sight of the canteens was punctuated on occasion with threats of reporting the canteen to the ministry for their poor performance of tea. When the critics realized that their guardian angels were not in government pay, complaints died and criticism was replaced by the official tea taster of each shelter. Their position was taken with a certain seriousness by everyone, including the overworked canteen volunteer who tried her (or his) best to provide the best sweetened tea allowed within the narrow limits of rationing. A sure sign that tea was particularly bad of an evening was when the tea taster remained silent after the first sip.

Look here, Steward, if this is coffee, I want tea; but if this is tea, then I wish for coffee.

Punch, 1902, vol. cxxiii

How effective tea was in saving lives—yes, in saving lives and sanity—was described succinctly in *Tea on Service* published for London's Ceylon Tea Centre in 1947. A thousand incendiaries followed by a bomb isolated a mobile canteen on its way home and many were injured and in shock. Ringed in by fire on three sides and the Thames on the fourth, the canteen workers and the injured had to wait until dawn for rescue. A constant kettle of water kept boiling for tea throughout the night was their only solace. There was no medical help within the group and yet none of the badly injured succumbed then or later. How much of a role the constant cups of sweetened tea played in saving any of those lives can only be conjecture. But the psychological benefits may have lessened the physical injuries. Who can say otherwise?

A favorite tale of the mobile canteens is the time a public house was bombed and the only survivor proved to be Jacko, the manager's tiny monkey. He was quickly given a few sips of very sweetened tea and then, because he was in shock, wrapped in blankets and laid flat. A passing police-man took pity on him, brought him a "real cup of tea"—meaning in a china cup—which the monkey promptly drank on his own, sitting up. The tea gone, he shook himself all over, turned around—and bit the policeman.

THE TEA VAN

Cousin of the city mobile canteen was an extraordinary vehicle which rumbled through the war. The tea van followed into battles, pulled up outside hospitals, alongside roads, next to camps, long enough to dispense cups and mugs of tea to patient, waiting lines of very tired men. Sponsored by different organizations—a Quaker group, the Salvation Army, Women's Volunteer Corps, a church group, etc.—the tea vans were never too far away from any soldier in any war circumstance. They bumped along mountain roads, disappeared in the desert dust, turned up at dockside as ships were about to pull out or come in, got stuck in snow and mud, and seemed to appear like magic when new numbers of casualties were returned from the front. They were ever present and that presence provided the security that so many men needed after hours, and sometimes days, of nonstop battle.

TEA SALUTED IN A DISPATCH

In a report to London concerning the routing of Field Marshall Erwin Rommel by the English:

> Our recovery troops also did well. It was quite common for the crew of a damaged tank to return the same night with their tank ready to fight again.
> Tea plays a big part in the desert fighting. "Let's have a brew" is a great expression in the desert. When a halt of twenty minutes is called, crews clamber from vehicles, a hole is dug in the ground, a twig fire is lit, and within ten minutes water is boiling in an old petrol tin. Tea, sugar and milk are added and the brew is ready within 15 minutes.

A SECRET CUP OF TEA

After Dunkirk (May 26–June 4, 1940), when the British were cut off from land escape by the Germans and were forced to retreat from the beaches into the waters, the Home Guard was organized. It seemed but a matter of time before Germany would invade Britain and the British would have to know how to keep on living with an invading army nearby. One of the three essentials in the training literally was the brewing of tea, making a cup of tea in the outdoors and but a short distance from an enemy force which had captured a village or outpost.

Rule 1. Never boil water during the day. The smoke is a dead giveaway.

Rule 2. Dig a hole one foot deep and build up the firewood. Begin with the bottom pieces as small as a match and the top ones no larger than a thumb. Follow the rules properly and the resulting fire will produce a glow without giving off flames visible in the night.

Rule 3. To get dry wood even during a thunderstorm, look for it on the trees. Dead twigs and dead branches are barely touched by the falling rain. The drops pass on down without soaking through the dead wood.

Rule 4. Sound carries. Do not snap off the twigs and branches. Deaden the noise by gloving one's hand or utilize a knife quietly.

TEA WITH THE AUSTRALIAN FORCES

From basic training camps to the front line, tea was a welcome, possibly essential part of the diet. If it is possible to be nuttier about tea than the British, then the blue ribbon would go to the Australians. It is almost their lifeline.

In rearward areas during the war, tea was served by the cooks at mealtimes—called *mess parades*. Tea was prepared in a large, oval, heavy metal container known as a *dixie* and, like its smaller cousin the billy, with a free-swinging handle. As some of the Australian troops regarded their cooks as a species of licensed poisoners, there was great joy among them when the poor man at the pot inadvertently picked up a dixie whose handle was hotter than he expected. (On one occasion in New Britain in 1944, such a cook was jumping up and down clasping his hands and moaning—after having run through a series of expletives—when one of his mess parade "victims" called out: "Was it heavy, Harry?")

The Blessed drink of early morning tea.

Jan Struther (Mrs. Joyce Maxton-Grahame) (1901–1953)
"Three Stockings"

In the fixed areas, where orderly lines could form, the cooks used ladles to dip the tea from the dixies into the tin pannikin (cup) carried by the troops. In forward situations, the troops generally carried their own individual, nonissue billies for tea-making. Empty fruit cans made ideal billies, made with a small wire handle along the lines of an out-back billy. The nonissue containers made good tea quickly over a minimal fire and doubled as a cup once the tea leaves had settled. Very lightweight, they could be hooked somewhere to the soldier's webbing, adding only ounces to the average seventy-eight pounds of gear he carried. Though the civilian population was on a strict ration basis, Australian troops were free of tea rationing throughout the war—unless, of course, something happened to the supply lines.

TEA AND THE BRITISH FORCES

It is just after dawn at an RAF airport "somewhere in England." An anxious group of men is waiting. Waiting. Some are pacing up and down outside the hangars, some are trying to keep their minds on other matters inside. Still others are looking into the skies, craning for a glimpse or a sound of planes overdue.

The planes have returned—perhaps all of them, perhaps less than the full flight that took off several hours earlier. The worn-out pilots are in the debriefing room, going over every single incident that occurred while notes are taken and their superiors listen. As they slowly unwind through the events of the night—the flight over the Channel, resistance encountered from enemy gunfire and aircraft, the amount of damage they were able to inflict on their targets, troubles they did not anticipate, areas that could not be reached—cups of tea are brought in. Hot, stiff and sweet cups of tea without which no intelligence reports would be complete. The imminent return of the planes always signaled time to put the kettle on.

These scenes have been incorporated into countless war movies involving British forces. But it is doubtful that anyone other than the British could ever appreciate the full impact of those cups of tea in similar or different war scenes.

*Though we eat little flesh and drink no wine,
Yet let's be merry; we'll have tea and toast;
Custards for supper, and an endless host
Of syllabubs and jellies and mince-pies,
And other such ladylike luxuries.*

PERCY BYSSHE SHELLEY, Letter to Maria Gisborne

The first thing offered survivors rescued from cold nights in open boats was tea. The last thing many flyers took before climbing into their plane was a hot cup of tea brought out on the field. Men on destroyers, including gun crews at station, got cups when they couldn't break for a meal. And after a sea battle if the ship and its men were still afloat, tea would appear magically, as if the cook had had nothing more important on his mind during the fighting than that his men should not miss their regular afternoon "cuppa."

Though tea was rationed throughout Britain and though the Royal Navy normally ran on provisions issued in allotted quantities, the First World War produced an exception. It was unlimited amounts of tea at sea and thanks are said to be due to Winston Churchill who was then First Lord of the Admiralty.

THE GERMAN TEA ALARM

One of the few pleasures to emanate from Germany during the war was listening to their propaganda broadcasts aimed at the British. Serious though their intent, they were received by most of their English audience as a joke and the direr the warnings of worse to come, the greater the jocular response.

Who decided the tea alarm is not known. It could have originated in the rococo offices of Hitler's minister of propaganda, Paul Joseph Goebbels. Or it might have just been the creation of the local station manager trying to show off his knowledge of English habits.

My experience . . . convinced me that tea was better than brandy, and during the last six months in Africa I took no brandy, even when sick, taking tea instead.

THEODORE ROOSEVELT (1858–1919), Letter, 1912

In any event, on the evening of October 4, 1939, thirty-one days after England and France declared war on Germany for invading Poland, the Zeisen radio station broadcast the following in a tone that might be reserved for announcing the imminent end of the world:

The high priests and priestesses of the cult of five o'clock tea in Britain are clamoring for an early peace. Their tea supplies from Java and China are running short. These high-class victims have been compelled to fall back on the coarser brand from India. The British people are slowly being convinced that Mr. Chamberlain's war is something worse than a temporary inconvenience.

How troubled were the British over such news was summed up best in a retort published the next day in the London *Daily Express*:

Sorry, Zeisen, but you've got it wrong. Four o'clock, not five, is tea time. And few of us in England drink China tea. And for those of us who do there are still tons and tons of China here.

135

*Tea
in War*

TEA IN THE FACTORIES

In a speech before the Works Management Association in London on September 18, 1940, Ernest Bevin, minister of labor in Churchill's coalition government (Churchill became prime minister earlier in the year) gave high praise to tea's role in factory production:

> I arranged with a great firm to carry out an experiment for me, because you have to move so much by trial and error. I asked them to adopt rigidly the hours I have set down in the circular I had issued: to give ten minutes break in the morning, ten minutes in the afternoon, with refreshment. The men had to work till seven at night and then there was a very long journey home, so I asked the management to send round barrows of tea at six o'clock in the evening and to see the result.

Bevin stopped, allowing his audience time to reflect upon his words. And then:

> Well, I would like you to see the curve of production, particularly in the last two hours. If a man has been in the habit of stopping at five o'clock, or five-fifteen, he goes home and he gets his meal just after six or about six-thirty. If he has got to work on, with nothing to eat—well, there is a sinking feeling and then when he travels home on a long road, there is a great proneness to cold and to infection, and that means absenteeism due to ill health. Now when that experiment I asked for had been going for a month, I asked a director of the firm if he wanted to give it up and he said, "Not on your life. I have made too much out of it because of the increased productivity."

Increasing company earnings had not of course been the motive behind Bevin's plan. But the point was well made. Within two years, more than ten thousand industrial tea canteens were on record. Before the war, workers took unofficial tea breaks whenever they could sneak them, management usually turning its back on the improvised methods employed for unscheduled rests. With factories running twenty-four hours a day during wartime to keep abreast of—if not ahead of—wartime demands, tea breaks came at different hours around the clock. Tea trolleys were pushed through the aisles of munitions factories, along shipyards and around huge aircraft assemblies. Tea bars were set up in ball-bearing shops, canteens in smaller work areas, while special wagons (a late-war model supplied eight hundred cups) covered work sites where men and women were deployed over a wide expanse.

No matter the time in which those breaks came, the few welcome moments away from noise, machines, concentration, hours of standing and numbing routine had far more positive consequences than even Bevin must have imagined possible. There is no doubt that tea was a definite—though unplanned—asset to the war effort. However, had a member of Parliament stood up before his peers at war's onset and predicted that tea would be Britain's "secret weapon" at home as well as on the fighting fronts, he would have been roundly dismissed and known forevermore as "that mad Parliamen*tea*rian."

THE ASSAM STORY

Within three months of Japan's attack on Pearl Harbor, she swept through the Pacific, taking the Philippines in January, Singapore in February and, on March 2, 1942, toppling the capital of Burma and sending the British and Indian armies into retreat through the jungle and back into India. Their hazardous route was compounded by weather, terrain and swarming Indian refugees ahead of them. Either they were soaked in rain or burnt by the sun as they struggled on foot twenty-five miles along a road whose elevations periodically dropped to almost sea level before rising to varying heights up to 5,700 feet. At its end, they finally had access to mobile transport for the last 160 miles of retreat.

The soldiers and refugees needed help in reaching India. Jungle tracks had to be cleared and supplies of food and medical equipment dropped at different places along the way of their return. There was no one available to do the job, so the British government asked the India Tea Association to assume responsibility. In early March 1942, the ITA Labor Force began with one tea planter and one hundred of his workers. By month's end, there were over twenty-eight thousand volunteers and in October the "Shadow Force" had swelled to ninety-five thousand.

At first they built roads out of the jungle and reception camps to receive the refugees while the association handled transportation, medical and rations problems entailed by their arrival. In 1943, when Britain was preparing her return to Burma, six thousand members of the Shadow Force joined with U.S. army engineers to construct oil pipelines, airfields, two roads—the two-hundred-mile Manipur and the eight-hundred-mile Ledo which led to China—and a supply base.

The volunteer force worked in harmony from its beginning. Had the British army taken charge of the wartime operations in Assam, it would have recruited all of the men from the estates and the gardens would have died. As it was, their running was left to a few remaining men, and the wives and children of the volunteers. Even under these limiting conditions, though maintenance of machinery and buildings suffered, the production of the tea leaves never did.

10

Tea Today

WHEN TEA WAS FIRST SOLD in European and British shops, it arrived at the grocers in the same chests as those in which it had been packed originally for shipment. The unblended teas, called "originals," were shipped in wooden chests lined with lead and soldered to prevent odor or moisture from creeping in. That was before the world discovered lead poisoning. Now they are shipped in plywood chests lined with rice paper and aluminum foil. Stamped on the top or side of the old chests was the name of the garden or estate from which the tea originated and that of the packer which, in time, came to mean something to both the grocer and his customer. By becoming familiar with the teas and the names of the different gardens, they grew to know which grades were of finer quality and which ones to ask for when either buying "straight" or having a blend made.

In those days—meaning before tea bag or even packaged loose tea— the blend was made up by the grocer as the order came over the counter. The tea chests were kept nearby and the teas spooned out, a little at a time, onto paper, mixed together and then wrapped up in the paper and sold. The method was slow and time never could have been of the essence on either side of the counter. Tortoise-slow though it would be considered today, it is another form of custom-buying—and one at its best—and certain grocers specializing in teas still maintain that quality of purchase even in this last quarter of the twentieth century. It is not unusual in such emporiums to find some of the loose teas showcased in tightly covered jars on the counter or stored in labeled tins within easy reach while the remaining teas stay packed in the chests until needed. "Originals" are not sold in any

Glass teapot forms
by Richard
Marquin. Late
twentieth century.
*Gallery for Fine
Contemporary
Crafts, New York.*

amounts comparable to the sales of blended teas for the very good reason
that most drinkers prefer the taste of their favorite tea to remain the same
each time it is bought. Such consistency is impossible with "originals" when
weather plays such an important role in tea's cultivation. The same weather
conditions would have to be guaranteed day in, year out.

It is possible to maintain consistency in blended teas through the sensi-
tivity and the expertise of the tea blender. "Originals" come from one
garden, but blended teas can be mixtures of teas from several gardens in
one district, such as Darjeeling, Assam, Ceylon or China, or tea mixtures
from different districts (different countries, too) such as Earl Grey, English
Breakfast or Irish Breakfast.

TEA'S JOURNEY

Left to grow wild, the evergreen tropical plant from which the tea leaf
comes, eventually grows into a tree thirty to fifty feet high and becomes
quite useless to tea production. To prevent that from happening, the plant
is cut back to no higher than four feet and, over a three-to-five-year period,
pruned and shaped repeatedly into a bush from which quantities of young
shoots grow. These shoots, called "flushes," produce two tender young leaves
and a small unopened bud which are used in the manufacturing of tea. The
picking or plucking of the shoots are done by hand, usually by a woman's
hand, moving with speed and lightness of touch to pluck and to toss the
shoots into tall baskets either tied to their backs or balanced on their heads.
Mechanical plucking has been considered and has been introduced, but it
cannot compare with or replace the gentleness of the hands of women who

Elephant teapot
by Coille Hooven,
1978. *Photo by
Tess Durgin.*

have been trained for their jobs since they were in their teens. The heavier work is left to the men.

At the day's end, the harvest of shoots is examined for stalks before being weighed. (An accomplished plucker can pick forty to forty-five pounds of shoots a day, enough to become ten pounds of salable tea.) The baskets of shoots are taken to the factory to be processed—large estates have their own factories, smaller ones send them to ones nearby.

The green leaves then go through several stages:

Withering. The leaves are thinly spread on shelves and left either to wither naturally or through heated air being forced over the withering racks. The point is to rid the leaf of as much water content as possible so that it will become soft and pliable.

Rolling. The leaves move from the racks to the rolling machinery which twist them and roll them to break up the leaf cells and free the juices so essential to the flavor. The first important chemical change originates during this process when the juices left on the leaf become exposed to the air and the development of the essential oil begins. The rolling twists the tea and the fine leaves drop through mesh sieves, are gathered up and taken to the fermenting room while the coarser leaves are rerolled.

Fermentation. The oxidation begun by the rollers continues in the cool fermenting rooms where the leaves are spread out on tile or cement floor or, perhaps, on glass tables to absorb the oxygen, turning them to the color of new copper. This process of oxidation distinguishes the black teas drunk by most Americans from green teas and prevents the blacks from being bought by Moslems whose religion forbids the use of any fermented product.

Porcelain teapot
by Elsa Rady,
1977.

Firing. This is also known as drying. Firing halts further oxidation of the leaves and allows them to dry evenly without being scorched. The leaves are placed on trays in an automatic tea drier, a large iron box, and as the trays move slowly up and down, continuous blasts of hot air hit the leaves. This does not mean that leaves are never overfired or scorched. Some are and, while one might think they would be packed off to the waste basket, that is not the case. They too go to auction, commanding far lower prices, and are used by blenders preparing cheaper blends. Ergo, scorched tea = cheap tea.

Once the leaves have gone through the drier they are ready to be graded and to take on one of several names, none of which convey quality but determine the size and appearance of the leaf. Basically, there are two main grades—leaf and broken leaf. The former comprise the larger leaves remaining after the broken ones are sifted out. They are Orange Pekoe, Pekoe and Pekoe Souchong (Pekoe is the English version of the Chinese symbol pronounced *pa-ho*, meaning *white hair* and referring to the white underneath the leaf).

The broken leaves include broken Pekoe, broken Orange Pekoe, broken Pekoe Souchong, Fannings (smaller leaves) and Dusts (not the dictionary term but the trade name for the smallest-size leaf which is valued for both its strength and quick infusion). The difference between the broken leaf grades is that the former, including Fannings, give a darker liquor with a stronger character than the leaf which generally yields more flavor and fragrance.

Green tea follows a different process of production. It is usually plucked without stalk and never withered or fermented, the leaf remaining green in color but lacking the aroma and flavor of the black. *Oolong*, the best quality grown in Taiwan, falls midway between black and green tea. It is slightly withered and then steamed to make the leaf pliable but to lessen fermentation and darkening. After slight fermentation, the leaves are rolled and fired, coming out a greenish-brown with a peachlike flavor. *Pouchong*, little known to the general public but preferred by the overseas Chinese and the wealthy Chinese, is neither green nor an Oolong, fermented in even less time than the Oolong and coming out as a slightly greener version of the Oolong. Many of the Pouchongs are scented with flowers but with the flower then taken out. The Jasmine is a Pouchong with the flower left in. (One New York blender uses it as his "secret" ingredient, listing the other teas used to make the blend, but not the jasmine flower.)

TEA AUCTION

Of the six tea auction centers around the world, five are called *primary auctions* and one is termed *in-transit*. The primary centers, where the tea auctioned has been grown in their country, are Calcutta for northern India; Cochin for southern India; Colombo, Sri Lanka; Jakarta, Indonesia; and Mombassa, Kenya, for east Africa. London, the in-transit market center, receives teas from all over which are sent on consignment and cataloged for sale.

Once the tea chests have been stored in special warehouses, weighed and marked, a small hole is bored in each and samples of the teas are made available to the tea brokers who, in turn, send smaller amounts to their clients who might be in Rotterdam, New York, Paris, Hamburg, etc. The brokers, as well as their clients, the importers, have their own tea sale rooms to which they repair with their expert tea tasters to carefully taste and evaluate the samples before placing their orders. The amount of tea that can be sold in one day is staggering—five million pounds is not uncommon.

A broker will often put a value on a specific chest, taking into account its weight, the time of year and how the tea was packed. Only certain operators can participate in the auctions although buyers' representatives are nearly always present just to watch or to communicate with their brokers in everchanging sign language should the need arise.

A long time ago, bids on a lot of tea lasted as long as it took an inch-long candle to burn out. The last bid heard as the room darkens is the one accepted. Romantic-sounding as that may have been, now the entire bidding on a lot can take place without a voice being raised, just a finger lifted to signal a quarter or half or full penny more bid on each pound. Because the tea buyers have had the chance to evaluate the teas before the Monday auction and relay their limits—if any—to their brokers, sales of each lot are accomplished in a matter of seconds. There is none of the tension and breath-holding associated with bids on antiques when an auctioneer is crying out, "Going, going, gone!"

The auctioneer usually opens with a price near or at his valuation of a given lot (which can number between twenty and sixty chests) and bidding speeds on. Occasionally, a lot might be bid on by several brokers willing to divide it in multiples of ten. However, if one tea has caught the fancy of a client, the broker may be unwilling to share the lot at all, or only allow a third of it to be bought. Once the sale is completed, the auctioneer announces the name of the buyer, how much tea was bought, how much it cost and everyone with a catalog notes name and figures accordingly.

THE BLENDING OF TEA

Overcoming the vagaries of Mother Nature is a science. But in the tea industry it is an art, one whose masters are the *tea blenders*. Tea, after all, is a natural product and, in its natural state, is subject to the stresses and caresses of the seasons, the impact varying the quality of leaves from the same bush weekly and seasonally.

To overcome that natural wrinkle and satisfy the demanding palates of customers for a particular tea (as yet no one has developed a seedling that will grow into an Earl Grey, English Breakfast, Orange Spice or Russian Caravan bush), the responsibility for consistency is left to the tea blenders. They must produce a uniform taste for each blend sold, a flavor that will not change from year to year regardless of whatever weather befell the tea plants.

At first thought, the assignment appears easy enough to fill. Follow the steps of the old-time grocer—take one part of this tea, one part of that, a little of a third, less of a fourth or more, mix well, put a little into a cup, pour on the just-boiled water, let steep, sip, nod or smile, jot down the formula and file for future reference and repeats. Would that it were that simple. Mother Nature's hand, however, is everpresent to change the formula and send the tea blender in search of similar teas from the same garden or district. At his fingertips, the tea blender has record books containing profiles of earlier successful blends, a vast stock of teas (numbering over a thousand) in the warehouse, and access to other supplies within the industry should his stock run low.

The highly professional blender or taster doesn't even need to taste the leaves to know their history. By picking up a few in his hand and feeling them with his fingers, he can tell when they were grown, where they grew (the district, the garden) and under what weather conditions they blossomed. But in the final frame, it is the blender's palate that determines the success of the blending, the seeming perfect duplication of a flavor. Depending upon the blends, as few as two or three different teas may be used or as many as fifteen, twenty, or even twenty-five. When a considerable amount of teas are used in a blend—as they are in the less expensive blends—one or two can be removed if need be without a noticeable change in flavor.

After the formula has been achieved on a small scale, it is ready to be duplicated in bulk quantities at the blending plant. The leaves—never

scribed number of times. (Too many times and the teas unmix.) Once
thoroughly blended, they go into hoppers which feed the packing machines.
They in turn feed the containers (or packages) with a prescribed amount
of tea, seal them and parcel them for distribution.

THE PACKAGING OF TEA

Tea bags developed quite by accident in 1904 when a tea merchant, anxious
to acquire new customers, sent out samples of his teas wrapped in small
silk bags. Not knowing how else to handle them—and assuming they were
doing the correct thing—a few of his customers put the bags in cups or
pots, poured on the boiling water and—presto—a new marketing idea was
born. Selling tea wrapped in silk was not a money-making venture and
silk soon gave way to a gauze material. Today's bags are neither of silk nor
of gauze but of a specially treated filter paper whose key ingredient is
abaca, strong yet flexible Manila hemp.

The packaging of teas is done entirely by machine, clickety-clacking as
they complete the process in a matter of seconds. It takes but one machine
to assemble the tea bag, from measuring the prescribed amount per bag to
filling the bag, sealing it and attaching string and tag.

Advertisement for
Salada Tea, 1920.
*Used with permis-
sion of the
Kellogg Company.*

A bank of machines handles the loose tea, taking a piece of cardboard, shaping it into a package, lining it with paper, filling it with measured loose tea, sealing and labeling it, and placing it on the conveyor belt. Instant teas, made from highly concentrated brews whose water has been removed by a drying process, are machine-measured and poured into glass jars and labeled. Iced tea, invented the same year as the tea bag but at the St. Louis World's Fair during a heat wave, has been made into a mix of instant tea, sugar and lemon flavoring poured into jars and pouches.

Whether the tea is loose or bagged, the most common form of packaging is cardboard containers wrapped in cellophane. The more expensive lines of tea can also be bought in decorative canisters or custom-made boxes, legends of the teas or the gardens from which they came inscribed on each. The fancy packaging, be it tea in an ironstone jar, tin canister duplicating another era or "the house caddy," usually surfaces at holiday time.

Rare is the grocer or supermarket who can afford to carry more than one of the higher price "name" teas, be it Twinings of London, Jackson of Piccadilly, or Fox Mountain Farms (of Louisiana). General consumer interest is still riveted on the generally lower-price tags of Tetley, Lipton, Red Rose, etc. But not even all of the general brands are found in every part of the country. Salada, for example, is sold in the East and in a few Western states, but not at all in the South. Southerners never took to Salada when they were given the chance.

TEA FLAVORS

The names of the blends may be the same but it does not follow that the components are alike. A case in point is the Earl Grey blend, an almost generic term today (when applied to tea). The original blend was presented to the second Earl Grey when he was in China the early part of the nineteenth century. A blend of the best China teas scented with oil of bergamot, it has a distinct but mild flavor. Other tea manufacturers produce their Earl Grey version today. Anyone can call a blend Earl Grey, but if it lacks a delicious hint of what one expects from an Earl Grey tea, the results will remain on the shelf, regardless of its name.

Some present-day Earl Greys are mixtures of the best India and Ceylon blacks scented with bergamot; of only Ceylon blacks and the oil scent; or, perhaps, a blend of Keemun and Darjeeling teas scented. Lapsang Souchong, which gives off a smoky, tarry flavor, is usually prevalent in all Earl Grey blends, but is not in Twinings' version. And, though Twinings holds the present Earl Grey under contract, Jacksons retains the original formula, a gift entrusted by the Earl to a Robert Jackson & Co. partner in 1830. As long ago as 1937, Jacksons announced they were selling a ton a week of the Earl Grey blend.

Sometimes, when a blend has been created specifically for a customer, it may in time—and with permission—be allowed to carry its name. The late Queen Mary is but one of these benefactors. The Queen Mary blend is made of fine broken Orange Pekoe teas from Darjeeling. The Prince of Wales blend (made for an earlier heir) is a leafy, bright-liquor tea blended from leaves grown in the Anhwei Province of China. Lady Londonderry's Mixture—a Jacksons exclusive—combines Ceylon, India and Formosa teas and was made for London's social and political hostess who lived during the first half of this century.

Both Twinings and Jacksons carry Russian-name teas. Twinings' Russian Caravan is a blend of teas from Anhwei Province and Oolong from Taiwan, said to have been a favorite of the Russian aristocracy and brought overland from China by camel caravan (it took sixteen months to complete the haul). Jacksons' Russian Tea is grown in the foothills of the Caucasian mountains, near the border of Turkey and Russia. Long leafed, it is in character and appearance not unlike some of the China teas.

In tea-cup times of hood and hoop
Or while the patch was worn.

ALFRED, LORD TENNYSON (1809–1892)
"The Talking Oak"

The Lemon Tea of Jacksons is a blend of Ceylon teas accented with lemon peel and lemon essence. Twinings' Spiced Tea is a mixture of Pekoe-leaf Ceylons blended with natural cut cloves and dried orange peel. Of the least known blends, Jacksons' Ching Wo is one. Delicately scented, it grows in Fukien Province, an area few Westerners have penetrated of late. Twinings' Green Gunpowder is one of the original historic China teas, its neat curled leaf similar in appearance to gunpowder, hence its name.

THE EFFECTS OF TEA

According to the redoubtable Prime Minister Gladstone: "If you are cold, tea will warm you. If you are heated, it will cool you. If you are depressed, it will cheer you. If you are excited, it will calm you."

Tea is a true stimulant. It is also a comforting drink, a security blanket on a cold night or after a long trip. It is also the ideal reviver *on* a long car trip. On the average, a cup of tea contains a little less than a grain of caffeine. When the tea is drunk, the caffeine is released gradually, the stimulating effect coming about fifteen minutes later. How much caffeine is in a cup depends on the strength of the tea brewed. China blends are generally lower in caffeine than the India blends, which run to darker color and stronger flavor (and which is why they are the preferred breakfast

In Boston, the #1 tea-drinking city, the #1 iced tea is Salada.

Did you know that Boston lies on the Blue Danube? It does in summer. That's when Johann Sebastian Bach moves over for Johann Strauss . . . when Boston Symphony makes way for Boston Pops . . . when Salada hot bows to Salada iced. Tonight, at intermission, when Mr. Arthur Fiedler here has lowered his baton on "Tales From the Vienna Woods," hundreds of thermos corks will pop merrily. Having iced tea on the grass at the Esplanade Concerts is considered

very Boston! But it's got to be the *proper* iced tea. Salada. You can really taste it through all that ice, because it contains more of the rich, expensive *Ceylon* tea leaves than other teas do. Bostonians like it—for the same reason they like good music. You don't live in Boston? You can find the same wonderful music on a Fiedler *record*—and the same Salada Tea in your store.

tea). When measured against coffee, a cup of tea generally contains about one-third of the caffeine in a cup of coffee, but, again, one must take into consideration the strength of each.

According to research data, the three pharmacologically important constituents of tea are *caffeine, theophylline* and *theobromine.* Caffeine's main effect is to stimulate the central nervous system and respiration. Theophylline has similar results but also produces muscle relaxation, diuresis, and coronary dilation and stimulates the heart. Theobromine acts in similar fashion, only to a lesser degree.

Tea also contains polyphenols, known as "tannin." Properly brewed tea should not contain any measurable amounts of it. If overbrewed, the tannin gives off a bitter taste. An old wives' tale claims that tannin "tans the inside of your stomach like leather," but it has yet to be proved, even though tea does stain the insides of pots and cups. Another old wives' tale warns that tea should never be drunk at a meal that includes meat. The argument is that the tannin will collide with the protein and render the meat indigestible.

Of all the times in the day, tea is probably most beneficial first thing upon waking. It is a tradition among the English of every class to have that cup of tea the moment one is awake. That early morning cup has a "buffering" effect on the stomach acids that have collected during sleep. Because of the quality of their strength, some blends are recommended as early morning teas, sold under various headings—English Breakfast, Irish Breakfast, Ceylon Breakfast. Milk is normally taken with early morning tea (ordinarily the tannin taste is always allayed by the casein in the milk added to tea). Tea with lemon is more conducive to evening time, though many people prefer lemon at all times to milk.

HOW TO BREW TEA

Tea should be made the way one prefers it but there are *basic rules* that should be followed. First, tea should always be kept in a tight container. If not, it loses some of its own delicate flavor and takes on extraneous smells.

The water to be boiled should be drawn cold from the tap and allowed the first roll of boiling. Under- or overboiled water deadens the brew.

While the water is boiling, the teapot—earthenware or china—should be warmed with hot water. Otherwise, the boiled water will lose its intensity and the flavor of the leaves will be released only partially. The teapot, by the way, should be waiting as close to the boiling kettle as possible. (Not so close that it might crack from the heat of the burner, but within arm's reach.) A wise saying is: "Take the teapot to the kettle, not the kettle to the teapot."

When using loose tea, one teaspoon of tea per person and one for the pot is the general rule of thumb. Allow the tea to steep between three and

Opposite: Advertisement for Salada Tea, 1960. *Used with permission of the Kellogg Company.*

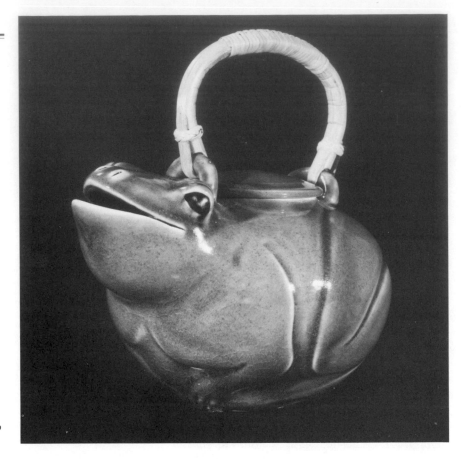

Ceramic hippo
teapot by Jenny
Lind, 1978. *Photo
by R. Faller.*

seven minutes. The longer time is required of the larger leafed teas. Normal time is about five minutes.

Follow the same brewing time for tea bags. And, when possible, keep the teapot hot with a "tea cozy" while the tea is steeping.

Iced-tea-making follows the same rules as those for hot tea, except that more tea should be used to counter the melting ice—about 50 percent more. Allow the tea to steep before pouring it into a pitcher filled with ice. Slices of lemon, sprigs of fresh mint and granulated sugar should always be served with iced tea (if available).

Iced tea can also be made with cold water. Fill a quart pitcher with cold tap water, add eight to ten tea bags (labels removed), cover, and let stand at room temperature or in refrigerator at least six hours, or overnight. Remove bags and pour into ice-filled glasses. That will make five to six glasses full.

How many cups of tea will a pound of tea make? As many as 200 cups, compared to 40 cups for a pound of coffee. The same proportion holds true for tea bags: 200 tea bags, 200 cups.

11

Serving Afternoon Tea

When Alice arrived for tea with the Mad Hatter and the March Hare (and with the Dormouse fast asleep between them), they cried out that there was no room at the table for her when obviously there was. The three simply had crowded together at one end, ignoring the rest of the table. Alice of course saw the true picture, pulled up an armchair and sat down at the end.

THE CRY TODAY is not that we lack room at the tea table for all who would share it. The plaint is that there is no room for afternoon tea in today's life-style, which runs with the speed of a computer and whose every day is as packed with activities as a memory bank with information. But if ever there were a time when time should be made for afternoon tea, it is now. The accelerated pace that has become the dictator and programmer of our lives, that pulls us along when we crave to stand still and catch our breath, can be slowed, can be broken.

That hour devoted to afternoon tea bespeaks a quiet, calm period, even when the tea table is set for ten. It is a time that serves as well in summer as in winter, indoors or out, an oasis of tranquility amid the devouring of time. It is a precious hour, minus mystique, that needs only to be experienced to be understood—and welcomed.

A formal tea is not a requisite to afternoon tea. As in the past, tea can be enjoyed around a kitchen table with only a slice of buttered toast to accompany it, or it can be served in the living room or the playroom, under a tree or up a mountain (ask any British climber), in an office or by the

Tea promotion:
"Favorite for
Brunch," 1975.
*Tea Council of
the D.S.A., Inc.*

"Mr. and Mrs.
Metayer drinking
tea." Silhouette by
J. A. Schmet-
terling, 1790.
*Ryksprentenkab-
inet, Amsterdam.*

side of a road. It matters not where the tea is taken, only that the hour be met wherever one is with a hot cup.

Afternoon tea in the classic English style contains certain formalities that should be observed. As a prelude to whatever evening plans may be on the guests' calendars, the best refreshments offered usually are the lightest ones.

The formal afternoon tea, beginning anywhere between 4:00 and 4:30 and lasting about an hour, can proceed two ways. When more than ten are expected, the table—be it the dining table or one in the living room—becomes the focal point to which guests gravitate. Covered in a linen cloth of white or ecru color, it may hold a tea service at one end and a coffee service at the other end. The tea service contains the teapot, hot water pot, sugar, small milk pitcher, strainer and a plate of thinly sliced lemons with lemon fork. The coffee service includes coffee pot, sugar and creamer. Cups, saucers and spoons are grouped together at each end with napkins,

"Lady at the tea table" by Mary Cassatt. *The Metropolitan Museum of Art, New York. Gift of the artist, 1923.*

and platters of thinly cut sandwiches, cookies and perhaps a cake are in between. A vase of flowers on the table provides a pleasing touch.

Friends of the hostess can be asked to pour the coffee and tea while she looks after her guests' enjoyment. Or, she might ask one friend to share the pouring chores with her. At the larger teas, guests usually stand

Tea in the Palm Court of the Plaza Hotel, New York.

as they do at cocktail parties, so sandwiches should be small and cakes and cookies easy to manage, obviating the need of a plate that must then be juggled with cup and saucer.

Informal teas are sit-down, guests numbering up to ten but preferably not exceeding five or six. A small table placed in front of the hostess will suffice to hold the tea equipage which now includes cake plates, knives and forks. Platters of sandwiches and cakes are placed on side tables, coffee table or desk, to be passed around by the hostess or an enterprising guest. At such teas, the food can include scones and crumpets coated in butter, gooier cakes and tarts and pots of jams.

Tea is best brewed on the strong side, to be diluted with hot water from the auxiliary pot. While a silver tea service may look more elegant on the table, porcelain pots hold the heat better. India and China teas are suitable for afternoon drinking and, in fact, at some homes both are offered. For the India tea, Ceylon Breakfast (a misnomer because it works well around the clock) or a good Darjeeling—Vintage, if price is no object. Of the China teas, Grey, China Black and Prince of Wales are among the most popular, while true connoisseurs may opt for such blends as Formosa Oolong, Lapsang Souchong, Jasmine and Russian Caravan.

*Indeed, Madame, your ladyship is very sparing of your tea;
I protest the last I took was no more than water bewitched.*

JONATHAN SWIFT (1667–1745)

The following pages contain a number of recipes. Some of them are for sandwiches and cakes to be served at afternoon tea and some are dishes in which tea is an ingredient. Of these, a few are also right for the tea table.

In preparing for an afternoon tea to which friends are coming, the important fact to remember is that the table does not need to be overloaded with food. Three different sandwich spreads are quite enough; an assortment of cookies and one cake (lemon in preference to chocolate) completing the table.

RECIPES

Using tea as a flavoring when preparing other foods is not as odd as it may sound at first. After all, coffee has been used often as an ingredient in recipes but, because of its subtlety, tea actually is compatible with a far wider range of food than is coffee.

Added to the cherry and pineapple pancake batter (recipe follows) it helps bring out the flavor of the fruit. It enhances the taste of the Indian

"Tea with milk and sugar to go, please." Fourteen-inch-high porcelain sculpture by Jan Axel, 1978. *The Elements, New York.*

kidneys and produces a smooth but rich sauce. It can add an unusual touch to homemade chutney, to an otherwise plain rice dish, to a salad dressing, even to breads and desserts and meats.

The following recipes have been culled from the files of and printed with permission from The Tea Council Limited, in London; Tea Council of the U.S.A.; and Twinings of London.

Breads and Cakes

COUNTRY TEA BREAD

Tea bread stays moist for about three weeks if stored in a tin with its lid on tight. Because it is sweetened with honey it will have a well-browned look.

7 oz. mixed currants, sultanas and seedless raisins	1 egg, beaten
1 oz. chopped orange peel	8 oz. self-raising flour
¼ pint prepared tea	salt
4 oz. clear honey	1 oz. butter, melted

Bread Topping:

honey	¼ oz. unrefined sugar
¼ oz. walnuts, chopped	

Put fruit, peel, tea and honey in bowl, cover and let stand overnight to allow fruit to swell and absorb tea flavor. Stir in the beaten egg, sifted flour, salt and melted butter. Transfer to a greased 1 pound bread tin and bake approximately 50 minutes at 350°. Take out, brush bread with honey, sprinkle sugar and walnuts on top, trickle more honey over nuts and sugar and return bread to oven. Bake approximately 20 minutes more.

Slice and serve with butter.

TEA SCONES

8 oz. self-raising flour	¼ pint strong cold tea
¼ tsp. salt	1 oz. butter
1 oz. sugar	4 oz. candied peel

Mix flour, salt and sugar in bowl. Add tea, then add buter and candied peel and mix into a soft manageable dough. Shape into a round on greased and floured baking sheet. Mark into 8 triangles with a knife and bake about 20 minutes in 375° until crisp and golden. Break into triangles as marked and serve immediately with butter.

KING'S ROW TEA CAKE

2¼ cups sifted all-purpose flour	½ cup (1 stick) soft butter or oleo
1½ cups sugar	1 cup cold Lemon Tea, double
3 tbsp. baking powder	strength
½ cup baking soda	1½ tsp. vanilla
½ tsp. salt	3 eggs

Frosting:

¼ cup soft butter or oleo	2 cups sifted confectioner's sugar
3 tbsp. cold Lemon Tea, double	
strength	

Mix flour, sugar, baking powder, baking soda and salt in a bowl. Add butter and ⅔ cup tea. Beat ingredients with electric mixer 2 minutes or until well mixed. Scrape down bowl and add remaining tea, vanilla and eggs. Beat for another 2 minutes until thoroughly blended. Pour batter into a greased and floured baking tin (13″ x 9″ x 12″) and bake in preheated oven 350°, 40 to 45 minutes or until brown and firm to the touch. Cool in tin.

Frosting: Mix ingredients in a bowl until smooth and fluffy. Spread lightly over top of cooled cake. Cut into squares and serve.

SPARE RIBS IN SWEET-SOUR GINGER SAUCE

2 lb. spare rib pork chops   1 tsp. salt
¾ pint prepared tea

Sauce:

2 oz. butter   2 oz. sliced stem ginger, chopped
1 large onion, peeled and chopped   salt and pepper
2 tbsp. cornflour   2 tbsp. flour
2 tbsp. vinegar   2 eggs, beaten
2 tbsp. soy sauce   4 to 5 tbsp. salad oil for frying
1 tbsp. sugar

Wash chops thoroughly. Put chops in large frying pan with tea and salt and bring to boil. Skim fat off top, lower heat and simmer ¾ hour. Remove chops from tea liquor and put in bowl. When cool, wrap in foil and refrigerate. Pour tea liquor into bowl, cool and then refrigerate to allow fat layer to rise to top and harden.

Before serving, cut porks into strips. Remove hard layer of fat from tea liquor and throw out. Melt butter in a pan, add onion and fry slowly until golden. Stir in cornflour and cook 2 minutes. Gradually blend in reserved tea liquor and bring to boil, stirring constantly. Add vinegar, soy sauce, sugar and ginger. Salt and pepper to taste. Allow to simmer over low heat while fixing meat.

Dip chops in flour and coat with beaten eggs. Heat oil in pan until hot but not smoking. Add meat and fry quickly until golden brown. Drain on paper. Serve immediately with flat noodles, the sauce and a chicory salad.

INDIAN KIDNEYS

2 tbsp. oil   salt and freshly ground pepper
1 large onion, sliced   ¼ lb. mushrooms, sliced
4 slices bacon, chopped   fresh mixed herbs of choice,
8 lamb kidneys   chopped
seasoned flour   ¼ pint heavy cream
½ pint prepared tea, cold

Heat oil in pan and sauté onion until transparent. Add bacon pieces and sauté 5 minutes.

Remove the core from the kidneys, wash and dry on absorbent paper. Coat kidneys in the seasoned flour, add to onion and bacon mixture and sauté 5 minutes. Add tea, bring to boil, season with salt and pepper to taste, add mushroom and herbs. Cover and cook 20 minutes. Just before serving, stir in cream, heat mixture through but do not allow to boil. Serve with rice.

1 slab bacon (about 1¾ lb.)
¾ pint prepared tea
1½ oz. butter
1½ oz. flour
3 heaping tbsp. cranberry sauce
¼ tsp. ground ginger
3 tbsp. heavy cream
½ tsp. Dijon mustard
1 tbsp. whiskey
salt and pepper

Put bacon slab in large saucepan and cover with cold water. Bring to boil and drain immediately. (This reduces possibility of excess saltiness.) Put bacon in clean pan, add tea and bring to boil. Skim fat off top of water, reduce heat and cover. Simmer approximately 1½ hours.

Remove bacon from tea liquor (reserve liquor). Cool bacon slightly before cutting into ½-inch cubes. Melt butter in clean pan, add flour and stir 2 minutes without browning. Gradually blend in tea liquor and bring to boil, stirring constantly. Add cranberry sauce, ginger, cream, mustard, whiskey and bacon cubes. Add seasoning to taste. Cover. Heat through gently about 15 minutes but do not allow to boil.

Serve with noodles and green vegetable (preferably broccoli or buttered spinach).

NOTE: *Bacon with Apricot and Walnut Sauce* may be made following the directions for the above recipe but substituting:
  2 oz. dried apricots, cut in small pieces
  2 oz. walnuts, shelled and chopped
for ginger and heavy cream ingredients, and:
  1 tbsp. port
for whiskey.

STUFFED DUCK WITH PINEAPPLE

1 oven-ready duck, about 5½ lbs.
2 bunches spring onions
1 pint medium strength prepared
  tea
syrup from 15½ oz. can of
  pineapple pieces (reserve pieces)
1 garlic clove
2 tsp. salt
3 tbsp. cornflour
3 tbsp. vinegar
2 tbsp. soy sauce
1 tbsp. sugar
1 medium onion (about 3 oz.),
  peeled and sliced
parsley

Remove giblet pack from duck and wash inside with cold water running through the cavity. Drain. Holding spring onions in their bunches, cut off a good third of the green ends and all the whiskery tops. Wash thoroughly without separating the bunches. Stuff in cavity of duck, pull loose skin over opening and secure with skewers.

Put duck into large pan containing tea, pineapple syrup, garlic and salt. Bring to boil. Lower heat, skim top off, cover pan and simmer gently 1½ hours. Lift bird carefully out of pan and allow to cool before wrapping in foil and refrigerating overnight.

Strain tea liquor from pan into a bowl and refrigerate overnight so that fat rises to surface. Allow duck to reach room temperature before roasting in 425° oven 30 to 40 minutes or until a deep golden brown.

Sauce: Remove fat from tea liquor and discard. Put tea in saucepan and heat but do not boil. Mix cornflour and vinegar till creamy and smooth. Add mixture to tea liquor. Add soy sauce, sugar, and sliced onion with rings separated. Bring to boil, stirring constantly. Cook, covered, *very gently* about 10 minutes.

Remove duck from oven and place on carving board. Garnish with pineapple pieces and parsley. Serve with sauce, green salad and long grain rice.

Relishes

APPLE AND DATE TEA CHUTNEY

4 lb. cooking apples
1½ lb. onions
2 garlic cloves, chopped
½ lb. stoned dates
½ pint strong prepared tea
1½ pints malt vinegar

1½ lb. granulated sugar
4 tsp. salt
3 tsp. ground ginger
1 tbsp. pickling spice (tied in a
    piece of muslin)

Peel, core and slice apples. Peel onions and cut up roughly. Peel garlic. Coarsely mince apples, onions, garlic and dates, put into large saucepan, add tea and bring to boil. Cover and simmer ½ hour. Add remaining ingredients except bag of spice and stir over low heat until sugar dissolves. Add spice bag and bring mixture to boil. Lower heat and cook slowly, uncovered, stirring frequently until chutney is the consistency of jam and is deep brown. It will take 2 to 3 hours. Cool in pan. Place in pot and cover. Makes about 4 pounds.

RHUBARB AND BANANA TEA CHUTNEY

½ pint strong prepared tea,
    strained
2½ lb. rhubarb (prepared weight),
    cut into 3-inch lengths
2 lb. onions, peeled and coarsely
    minced
2 garlic cloves, peeled and chopped
1½ lb. granulated sugar

2 tsp. ground ginger
3 tsp. salt
4 ripe bananas (1¼ lb.),
    peeled and sliced
1½ pints malt vinegar
½ lb. currants, washed
1 tbsp. pickling spice (tied in
    muslin)

Put prepared tea into large, heavy saucepan, add rhubarb and cook until rhubarb is soft. Add remaining ingredients except spice bag. Stir over low heat until sugar dissolves. Add spice bag and slowly bring to boil. Lower heat and cook slowly, uncovered, 2 to 3 hours, stirring frequently until chutney is consistency of jam and is a deepish brown. Cool in pan, place in pot and cover. Makes about 4 pounds.

Casseroles

FRENCH-STYLE MEAT AND BEAN HOT-POT

1 lb. uncooked butter beans	2 to 4 garlic cloves, peeled
3 lb. belly of pork	and chopped
2 lb. neck of lamb	extra salt
2½ pints medium strength	freshly milled pepper
prepared tea, strained	1 tsp. marjoram (or mixed herbs)
2 to 3 tsp. salt	4 heaping tbsp. lightly toasted
3 large onions, peeled and	breadcrumbs
left whole	

In bowl place beans and cover with 1 pint hot tea. Cover and soak overnight.

Wash meats under cold running water and place in large saucepan. Add the tea, onions and salt and bring to boil. Remove film, lower heat, cover and simmer ¾ hour. Remove meat and onions from pan. Cut pork belly into slices and place both meats with onions on a plate. Cover. Pour tea liquor into bowl and refrigerate overnight to allow fat to form hard layer on surface. Refrigerate meats and onions overnight too.

Following day, place onions in large casserole, followed by alternating layers of butter beans (and any unabsorbed tea) and meats. Sprinkle garlic, salt, milled pepper and marjoram between each layer. Remove hard film of fat from tea liquor and discard. Heat up liquor with remaining ½ pint tea. Pour into casserole over beans and meat. Sprinkle thickly with breadcrumbs, cover tightly and cook in lower part of 325° oven 2½ to 3 hours.

Serve with green salad.

SPICED TEA GLAZE FOR HAM (enough for a 5-lb. smoked ham)

1 tbsp. Spiced Tea or 3 tea bags	⅓ cup maraschino cherries, chopped
½ cup boiling water	1 tbsp. cornstarch
1 cup pineapple preserves	5-lb. half smoked ham

Steep tea in boiling water 5 minutes, then strain. In pan, mix tea, preserves, cherries and cornstarch and cook over low heat, stirring constantly, until glaze thickens. Spoon about ⅓ of the glaze over the ham. Roast in preheated 350° oven 30 minutes, remove from oven and spoon ⅓ more of glaze over ham. Return to oven and bake another 30 minutes. Repeat this process with final ⅓ of glaze and roast 30 minutes more. Cut ham into thin slices and top each slice with some of the pan juices.

Vegetables

STEAMED SAVORY RICE

½ oz. margarine
1 onion, diced
1½ cups long grain rice
1 tsp. turmeric

1 tsp. bouquet garni
1 cup tea
½ tsp. salt

Melt margarine in pan and sauté onions and rice about 5 minutes. Add turmeric and herbs, stir well. Add tea and salt, cover pan, and steam on lowest heat possible about 30 minutes or until rice is cooked but still a little firm.

Potatoes

HOT YAM SOUFFLE

3 24-oz. can yams, drained or
8 medium-size fresh yams, cooked
    and peeled
2 tbsp. Spiced Tea (or 6 tea bags)
1 cup boiling water

3 egg yolks
1 cup apricot preserves
¼ cup melted butter
3 egg whites, stiffly beaten

In large bowl, mash yams until smooth. Steep tea in boiling water for 5 minutes, then strain into yams. Add egg yolks, preserves and butter. Beat until smooth and well blended. Fold in egg whites. Spoon mixture into a buttered 3-quart casserole. Bake in preheated 350° oven 60 minutes or until puffed and golden brown.

The family drinking tea at suppertime. Cover for booklet "What You Should Know About Tea." *Tea Council of the U.S.A., Inc.*

Spiced Salad Dressing

1 tbsp. Spiced Tea (or 3 tea bags)
½ cup boiling water
1 cup plain yogurt

¼ cup honey
1 tsp. grated lemon rind
1 tbsp. lemon juice

Steep tea in boiling water for 5 minutes, then strain. Allow to cool. In mixing bowl, fold in yogurt and stir in tea. Stir in honey, lemon rind and lemon juice and stir some more. Chill until ready to serve. Good over fruit, ham, chicken, turkey and cottage cheese. This recipe yields 1¾ cups.

Desserts

Spiced Tea Chiffon Pie

1 cup graham cracker crumbs
2 tbsp. sugar
½ cup melted butter or margarine
2 tbsp. Spiced Tea or 6 tea bags
2 cups boiling water
½ cup sugar

2 envelopes unflavored gelatin
2 egg yolks
2 egg whites, stiffly beaten
½ pint heavy cream, whipped
garnishing: additional whipped
    cream and orange slices

In bowl, mix crumbs, sugar and butter or margarine. Press mixture evenly into the bottom and sides of ungreased 9-inch pie pan. Chill.

Steep tea in boiling water 5 minutes and drain. In bowl, mix sugar and gelatin. Stir in hot tea until gelatin dissolves. Beat in egg yolks. Chill mixture until syrupy. Fold in egg whites and whipped cream, pour mixture into pie shell and chill until firm. Garnish with whipped cream and orange slices.

Tea Charlotte

1½ lb. cooking apples
1 lemon
4 cloves
½ pint tea
3 tbsp. honey

1 tsp. arrowroot
2 oz. raw peanuts
2 oz. butter
6 oz. fresh breadcrumbs, browned

Peel and slice apples and place in oven-proof dish. Grate lemon peel and reserve. Squeeze lemon juice over apples. Sprinkle cloves over apples.

Warm tea together with 1 tablespoon honey. In separate bowl, blend arrowroot with a little tea and add to tea and honey mixture. Bring to boil, stirring constantly, until mixture thickens. Pour over apples.

Chop nuts well. Melt butter in saucepan and sauté nuts one minute. Add remaining honey, breadcrumbs and grated peel, mix well. Spoon on top of apples and bake in preheated 350° for 35 minutes.

Frozen Tea Mousse

1 envelope unflavored gelatin
¼ cup cold water
½ cup sugar
1 cup hot Lemon Tea, strong

1 pint heavy cream, whipped
1 15-oz. can apricot halves,
    drained and diced

Mix gelatin in cold water. Mix sugar and hot tea in separate bowl and stir in dissolved gelatin. Continue stirring until slightly thick. Fold in whipped cream and apricots. Pour mixture into freezer container, cover and freeze until hard. To serve, scoop or spoon into chilled serving dishes. Garnish with additional apricots if desired. Serves 8.

Cherry and Pineapple Pancakes

4 oz. plain flour
salt
1 egg
½ pint cold prepared tea
oil or margarine for frying

juice of 1 lemon
black cherry jam
1 small can pineapple rings
¼ pint heavy cream

Sift flour and salt in bowl. Add egg and mix into dry ingredients. Gradually add tea, beating well between each addition.

In frying pan, heat a little oil or margarine and quickly pour in about 2 tablespoons of the batter and make pancakes the usual way. Sprinkle each

Tea flyer for six flavors. *First Colony Coffee & Tea Company, Inc.*

pancake with lemon juice and spread over with the black cherry jam. Roll up pancakes and place in ovenproof dish. Cut pineapple rings in half and arrange over pancakes. Pour the cream over the pancakes.

Place dish with pancakes under broiler and allow cream to bubble and brown lightly before removing. Serve immediately.

Sandwiches and Cakes for Afternoon Tea

DEVILED CHIVE SANDWICHES

1 (2¼-oz.) can deviled ham
1 cup cottage cheese
1 tbsp. chopped chives
salt and white pepper

12 thin slices whole wheat bread,
    buttered and trimmed
lettuce, washed and dried

Combine deviled ham, cheese, chives, salt and pepper to taste in bowl and mix well. Spread half the bread slices with mixture. Place lettuce over spread and top with remaining bread slices. Cut each sandwich into four triangles or squares.

KUMQUAT FINGER SANDWICHES

2 8-oz. packages cream cheese
2 tbsp. milk

16 slices thin whole wheat bread
2 8-oz. jars preserved kumquats

Allow cream cheese to come to room temperature, then whip with milk and spread on bread slices. Trim crusts and cut each piece into three strips. Drain and slice kumquats and place several slices on each sandwich finger. Makes 48 sandwiches.

POTPOURRI OF SANDWICHES

2 8-oz. packages cream cheese
¼ cup heavy cream
3 tbsp. minced crystalized ginger
3 tbsp. minced parsley
¼ tsp. Tabasco sauce

3 tbsp. drained capers
12 slices thin white bread
12 slices thin rye bread
12 slices thin whole wheat bread
watercress

Bring cheese to room temperature and blend well with cream. Then divide into 3 equal portions. Blend ginger into first portion, parsley and Tabasco into second portion and capers into the third one. Make six sandwiches with white bread and ginger mixture, six with rye bread and parsley mixture and six with whole wheat bread and caper mixture. Wrap all well with waxed paper or foil and refrigerate until well chilled. When ready to serve, trim crusts from white sandwiches and cut each into four triangles; trim rye sandwiches and cut each into four fingers (four strips); with small cookie cutter, make four circles from each whole wheat sandwich. Place on large platter and decorate with watercress. Makes 72 sandwiches.

TOMATO TEA SANDWICHES

3 medium-ripe tomatoes　　　　12 slices thin white bread
mayonnaise　　　　　　　　　　salt

Slice tomatoes as thin as possible. Spread mayonnaise on 6 slices of bread. Place tomatoes over mayonnaise. Salt to taste. Spread mayonnaise on remaining 6 slices, cover tomatoes. Trim sandwiches and cut into triangles. Makes 18 sandwiches.

CREAM CHEESE AND WATERCRESS SANDWICHES

2 8-oz. packages cream cheese　　18 slices white bread, trimmed
1 large bunch watercress　　　　additional watercress

Allow cream cheese to come to room temperature. Chop watercress leaves finely and put in bowl. Add cream cheese and mix well. Spread cheese mixture on each of the bread slices. Roll each slice and place on platter. Garnish with additional watercress. Makes 18 sandwiches.

ALMOND TEA CRESCENTS

1 cup butter, softened　　　　　½ tsp. almond extract
1 cup confectioner's sugar, sifted　1¾ cup unsifted all-purpose flour
2 tsp. instant tea　　　　　　　½ cup finely chopped almonds

Cream butter in bowl. Gradually add sugar and beat until light and fluffy. Blend in tea and almond extract. Gradually mix in flour, then almonds. Mix well and refrigerate 2 hours or more until well chilled.

Shape the dough, a teaspoon at a time, into small crescents. Place one inch apart on ungreased cookie sheet. Bake in preheated 350° oven until lightly browned (about 15 minutes). Cool briefly but, while still warm, dust lightly with confectioner's sugar.

MARTHA'S GREAT CAKE (adapted from a recipe of Mrs. George Washington)

1 cup butter　　　　　　　　　¼ cup brandy
1 cup sugar　　　　　　　　　　2 8-oz. jars ready-to-use fruits
5 eggs　　　　　　　　　　　　　and peels
2½ cups sifted flour　　　　　　2 8-oz. jars ready-to-use whole
¼ tsp. nutmeg　　　　　　　　　cherries

Cream butter in bowl and add sugar gradually. Beat until light and fluffy. Add eggs, one at a time, beating well. Stir in about half the flour, sifted with the nutmeg. Add brandy and remaining flour and blend gently, but well. Stir in fruit. Turn into ungreased 9-inch springform ring mold or 9-inch tube pan with removable bottom. Bake in 300° oven for about 80 minutes or until top is golden brown and springs back when touched gently with the finger. Cool in pan on rack for about 30 minutes. Remove from pan and allow to cool another 15 minutes before serving.

LANE CAKE

1 cup butter or margarine	1/16 tsp. salt
2 cups sugar	8 egg whites
3¼ cups sifted cake flour	1 cup milk
2 tsp. double-acting baking powder	2 tsp. vanilla

Allow butter or margarine to come to room temperature in bowl. Add sugar and cream butter with sugar until light and fluffy.

In separate bowl, sift flour together with baking powder and salt. Add egg whites, one at a time, to sugar mixture, beating well after each addition. Fold in flour mixture alternately with milk mixed with the vanilla, beginning and ending with the dry mixture.

Pour into four ungreased 9-inch layer pans whose bottoms are lined with waxed paper. Bake in preheated 375° oven about 20 minutes or until the edges shrink slightly from sides and the tops spring back when pressed gently. Cool in pans on racks about 5 minutes. Remove from pans, invert on racks and remove wax paper. Turn right side up and finish cooling. Fill and frost.

Filling:

8 egg yolks	1 cup seedless raisins, finely
1 cup sugar	chopped or ground
½ cup butter or margarine	⅓ cup bourbon or brandy
	1 tsp. vanilla

Beat egg yolks well in 2-quart saucepan. Beat in sugar and butter which has softened at room temperature. Cook over moderate heat, stirring constantly, until quite thick. Remove from heat Add raisins, bourbon and vanilla and blend well. Cool a bit before spreading evenly onto first three cake layers. Stack carefully and top with fourth layer. Frost entire cake.

Frosting:

½ cup sugar	2 tbsp. water
¼ cup white corn syrup	2 egg whites, well beaten
⅛ tsp. salt	½ tsp. vanilla

Put sugar, syrup, salt and water in 1-quart saucepan. Boil over moderate heat until syrup spins a thread (or cooking thermometer reaches 242°). Gradually beat half the syrup into the beaten whites. Place remaining syrup in pan of hot water to keep warm. Continue beating until syrup/egg-

Afternoon tea,
sandwiches, wafers,
and cake. *Tea
Council of the
U.S.A., Inc.*

white mixture is thick and fluffy. Add remaining syrup and vanilla and
continue beating until mixture holds stiff and shiny peaks. Swirl onto sides
and top of cake.

LEMON POUND CAKE

¼ pound butter
½ cup Crisco
2 cups sugar
3 eggs
3 cups flour

½ tsp. baking soda
¼ tsp. salt
1 cup buttermilk
1 tsp. lemon juice
1 tsp. lemon rind

In bowl, cream butter, Crisco and sugar. Add eggs and beat well. In
separate bowl, sift flour, soda and salt. Add to butter mixture alternately
with buttermilk, beginning and ending with dry mixture. Beat well. Add
lemon juice and lemon rind and beat well again.

Bake in greased tube pan about 325° for 60 minutes or until top springs
back when touched lightly. Allow to cool before removing from pan to be
iced.

Icing:

¼ pound butter

1 box confectioner's sugar

juice and rind of 2 lemons

1 package of coconut shreds

Allow butter to soften at room temperature in bowl before mixing in sugar. When blended well, add the juice and rind of 2 lemons. Mix well. Cover cake. Sprinkle coconut shreds on top.

Tea Drinks

CIDER TEA

2 qt. fresh cold water

15 tea bags (or ⅓ cup loose tea)

1 qt. apple cider or apple juice

2 tsp. grated lemon rind

¼ cup lemon juice

½ cup sugar

In saucepan, bring water to full rolling boil. Remove immediately from heat, add tea, and steep 5 minutes. Strain into a large pitcher and stir a couple of times. If serving cold, add cider or juice and other ingredients. Cool to room temperature and pour over ice cubes. If serving hot, heat cider or juice and add to the hot tea along with other ingredients. Use lone cinnamon sticks as stirrers (optional).
Makes 12 to 16 servings.

HALAKAHIKI TEA

1 qt. boiling water

15 tea bags (or ⅓ cup loose tea)

2 tbsp. dehydrated mint leaves or
   4 tbsp. fresh mint

1 qt. cold water

1 cup lemon juice (4 to 5 lemons)

⅔ cup sugar

¾ cup (6-oz. can) pineapple juice

12 fresh pineapple spears

Pour boiling water over tea and mint leaves in pan. Cover and allow to cool 5 minutes. Strain into pitcher containing quart of cold water. Add lemon juice, sugar and pineapple juice. When ready to serve, place a pineapple spear in each glass, add ice and pour in tea. Garnish with fresh mint (optional). Makes 12 servings.

ORCHARD TEA

1 part Darjeeling Tea

1 part apple juice

1 apple, thinly sliced

Brew tea before pouring through strainer into pan and adding like amount of apple juice. Heat but do not allow to boil. Pour into cups or mugs and serve with apple slice floating on top.

(Recommended for mid-morning or afternoon break, summer or winter.)

With and without
mint. *Tea Council
of the U.S.A., Inc.*

BLACK RUSSIAN

1½ pt. tea
4 tbsp. lemon juice
4 tbsp. extra-fine granulated sugar
3-inch stick cinnamon

4 cloves stuck into a length of
    lemon peel
1 pint red wine
1 lemon, sliced

Heat together all the ingredients except the lemon slices. Strain into tall glasses and garnish with lemon slices. Serves 6.

PLANTER'S TEA

2 pt. strong tea
1 pt. dark rum
½ pt. orange juice

¼ pt. lemon juice
soft brown sugar to taste
small pieces of orange and lemon

Heat prepared tea, rum, orange and lemon juice until hot, but do not allow to boil. Sugar to taste. Pour into mugs and garnish with lemon and orange slices. Serves 10.

APRICOT WINDJAMMER

1 cup prepared tea

1 tbsp. apricot puree (baby food is all right) or 2 tsp. sieved apricot jam

sugar to taste

heavy cream (optional)

Steep tea before adding apricot puree or jam. Stir well, add sugar to taste. Add cream if desired. Serves 1.

EVENING MIST

3 oz. prepared tea

2 oz. whiskey

3 tsp. clear honey

heavy cream (optional)

Heat prepared tea, whiskey and honey but do not allow to boil. Pour into demitasse cups and top with heaping spoonful cream.

ON GIVING A TEA-TASTING PARTY

Tea is tea and all teas taste the same, mutters the skeptic. But tea connoisseurs know that that isn't so. How to convert the skeptic? One way—an entertaining way—would be to host a tea-tasting party, perhaps making the skeptic the guest of honor. The idea is novel enough to attract considerable curiosity among friends, it is low in calories—unless sandwiches and cakes are served afterward—and inexpensive to give. It is also fun, particularly when watching the face of the skeptic and the look of astonishment that frequently comes when the realization dawns that tea is not just tea, no matter what.

How does one give such a party and when should it be held? Any time is all right, really, providing it isn't right after a meal. The best time of course would be in the afternoon around tea time.

The three basic tea types—green, brown and black—should be included at a first tea-tasting party. Focus on more selective teas can be given with one's advancement as an amateur tea taster.

As mentioned earlier, all tea as we know it today is fired, or heat-dried, tea. Brown tea—such as Formosa Oolong—is only partially fermented before firing; green tea, the most ancient of the three and the one still used in the Japanese tea ceremony, is made of leaves not fermented before firing; while black tea, the one Westerners know best, is completely fermented before firing. The degree of fermentation makes an important difference in the "final flavor" of the tea leaves.

Of the three types, black has the greatest number of subvarieties, with China blacks usually considered the most delicate. Among these teas are the traditional Chinese "court" tea sold under the name of China Black, Prince of Wales and Russian Caravan. Jasmine tea is black but mixed with jasmine petals; Lapsang Souchong is black with a smoky flavor.

The black teas of India vary from the mellow, large-leaf Darjeelings grown in the cooler hill country to the bright-flavored leaves of Sri Lanka (used in such blends as Orange Pekoe and Lemon), and the small, full-bodied leaves of southern India which make the hearty teas, such as Assam and Irish Breakfast.

The quality of the tea leaves vary considerably with the tea garden in which they grew, the vagaries of weather and the relative youth of the leaves when plucked.

Armed with this knowledge, the tea-tasting host should be ready to proceed with the tasting, the directions for which are not unlike those for wine-tasting. The tasting should begin with the mildest blend and progress to the stronger ones. One important reminder—smoking in the room or by anyone participating in the tasting should be forbidden until after the tasting is completed. Light refreshment, however, can be included, to have with the tea and to clear the palate. Biscuits, a plain cake or tea sandwiches will do, providing their taste is mild enough not to compete with or overpower the taste of the teas.

A tea-tasting table should be set with a sugar bowl, milk pitcher, a dish of sliced lemons, spoons and a tea strainer. Each blend of tea should steep in its own pot, made from fresh boiling water (do not reboil the water used for the previous blend).

For her own breakfast she'll project a scheme,
Nor take her tea without a stratagem.

EDWARD YOUNG (1683–1765), *Love of Fame*, Satire I

The water should be poured into the warmed teapots, each one holding a spoon's worth of leaves for each person tasting it. The teas should steep in the pot three to seven minutes—less for the smaller-leaf teas, longer for the larger leaf. To serve the tea, the cups should be half-filled and a minute allowed for the tea to cool a little before sipping it. It is more important to sip the tea than to swallow it. Sip only a slight amount, allow the flavor to be savored and then swallow it. This gives the taste a chance to establish itself and, with experience, to be more easily identified. Guests should then be asked to add milk or lemon and sugar, if desired, to compare the intensity of the flavor that comes through with these additions with that present when the tea was plain (or "neat" as the British say).

With the serving of each new blend, guests should be told which one they are tasting. One way to remember is to attach a tag to each pot. An added bonus to the tea-tasting is to tell a little of the tea's origin, after which comparison could be made between the dry leaves in their original caddy or container and the unfurled leaves in the teapot.

Four to six tea blends are enough to consider for a bona fide first tasting. With four, the selection might be Lapsang Souchong, Prince of Wales, Earl Grey and English Breakfast; with six, Prince of Wales, Lapsang Souchong, Formosa Oolong, Earl Grey, Vintage Darjeeling and Spiced Tea.

Tea-tasting can be approached in a number of ways with different "themes" deciding the focus. One tasting might rely on the breakfast teas, using a sequence of Ceylon Breakfast, English Breakfast, Assam and Irish Breakfast. In this instance, buttered toast and muffins would be added to the table for later eating.

A tasting with a historical perspective on tea would begin with the green tea (Green Gunpowder) which may be as old as five thousand years and proceed to the China blacks and browns (China black and Formosa Oolong), in use about fifteen hundred years. The next cups would be filled with Assam or Irish Breakfast (the first good crops harvested in 1839), a Darjeeling cultivated soon afterward and a Ceylon (Ceylon Breakfast or Orange Pekoe), first available in 1875. The tasting would finish with the relatively new-flavored Ceylons, possibly Lemon and Spiced Tea.

For a tasting devoted to China teas, begin with Green Gunpowder and

Tea caddies. *Museum of Fine Arts, Boston, Massachusetts.*

proceed to China Black, Russian Caravan, Formosa Oolong, Jasmine, Prince of Wales, Lapsang Souchong and Earl Grey. A really advanced taster might attempt to hold a tasting with other more advanced guests and attempt to detect the nuances of three different blends of Darjeeling—Darjeeling, Queen Mary (blended originally for the Queen who later gave permission for it to be named after her) and Vintage Darjeeling.

An added postscript on the tasting itself: Professional tasters do not swallow the tea they taste. The little that they sip from each cup is rolled around in the mouth a few times while the flavor is established and then it is spit out. While that is normal procedure for a professional, it may not appeal to the amateur tasters in a private home. The best alternative is to sip a spoon's worth of tea, savor it, then swallow it. In order not to confuse the palate with the different tastes, cleanse the palate between sips with a sip of water.

SURPRISING (AND NOT SO SURPRISING) TEA TIPS

According to The Tea Council Limited in London, tea has many applications beyond that of being a good drink. It can serve in household chores and in health care, as witness the following:

Herbal Tea Face Steamer

To remove impurities from the skin, place face (with towel held over head to retain escaping steam) over bowl of very hot (and freshly made) tea to which have been added strips of lemon rind, marjoram and mint.

Foot Bath

Bathe feet in bowl of cold tea to which juice of one lemon and pinch of salt have been added.

Skin Tonic

Dip swab of cotton in cold tea, dab on skin and allow to dry.

Sty in Eye

Soak cotton wool in cold (or warm) tea and place over eye. Repeat frequently.

Tea makes an excellent mulch for roses. Used tea leaves placed over roots of rose bushes helps soil retain moisture and helps feed the plant.

Left-over tea liquid poured over houseplants helps stimulate growth.

Household Uses

Floor cleaner: When sweeping concrete floor (as in garage or workshop), sprinkle first with used tea leaves. Dirt and dust will adhere to leaves instead of rising into air when swept.

Lace mats or cream-colored materials can be rinsed with tea to give them their original cream tint after fading from use.

Additional Food Uses

Substitute cold tea for half the liquid required in rich cake mixtures to give good color and subtle flavor.

Iced tea cubes: Make a pot of tea, strain into jug after cooled and sweeten to taste. Pour tea into ice tray and place a peeled grape or a strawberry into each cube section. Freeze. Use cubes to accent cold tea drinks or decorate punches. This will cool the drink without diluting it as ice would.

Add slices of cucumber to iced tea for a refreshing drink on a particularly hot day.

Soak and cook dried apricots in tea to vary and improve their flavor.

It frequently breakfasts at five-o'clock tea,
And dines on the following day.

LEWIS CARROLL, "The Hunting of the Snark," Stanza 17

Tea by Mail

FOR THE DEDICATED TEA LOVER the best of all worlds is a tea shop, a shop brimming with chests of teas from which to make up blends, and shelves lined with caddies containing a wide selection of straights and blends—and labeled with exotic names. Unfortunately, those shops are not on everyone's Main Street, but there is an alternative to supermarket shelves—ordering by mail. Whether coming from England or India or Sri Lanka, or from a specialty house in the United States, most have brochures at hand to quote present prices, and can be sent immediately.

Please remember that though similar names of blends will appear in the following list, it does not mean that each tea—be it the Earl Grey or the Breakfast Tea or the Russian Caravan or another—will taste identical. Each has its own formula within the overall concept.

Connecticut

CRABTREE & EVELYN, LTD., BOX 167, WOODSTOCK HILL 06284

At present, the company offers six different teas in packages of twenty-four sachets (sachets is another word for tea bags). In time, these teas will also be sold loose in larger weights. Crabtree & Evelyn also plans to have sixteen or more flavored teas blended in West Germany. The special blends will be completely naturally flavored (so many of the flavors are synthetic).

Teas sold in the individual packaging at present include Broken Orange Pekoe, Darjeeling, Earl Grey, Formosa Oolong, China Jasmine and Keemun

Tea caddy.
Thauvet Besley, fl.
1727–1757.
Initialed "CMP"
on base for Cath-
erine McPhaedres
(married Robert
Gilbert Livingston
in 1740). Initialed
"CLR" for
Catherine Living-
ston Reade, their
granddaughter.
Gift of Miss
Margaret Stuy-
vesant Dart.
*Museum of the
City of New York.*

English Breakfast. (In England they might say Keemun is one kind of tea,
English Breakfast another. But in America it is KEB all the way.) Prices
run from $2.00 to $2.25 a package, plus postage.

O. H. CLAPP & CO., INC., 42 RIVERSIDE AVENUE, WESTPORT 06880

A tea importer, Clapp & Co. decided to expand its role by offering vintage
teas to mail-order customers. Packed in attractive miniature wooden chests,

the teas are sold in five- and eight-ounce weights, depending upon leaf size. The teas are Formosa Oolong, Keemun, China Jasmine, Darjeeling (coupled with the flavor of black currant), Rose Congoo (scented with rose petals) and Oolong. Price is $7.50 a chest.

Clapp & Co. suggests that those trying China Jasmine for the first time should follow an ancient Chinese proverb—the second cup, or the second brew, is often better than the first. After the teapot is empty of the liquid, pour fresh boiling water over the *same*—repeat, the *same*—tea leaves. The second pot will be less imposing.

California

EAST INDIA TEA & COFFEE CO., LTD., 1481 3RD STREET, SAN FRANCISCO 94107

The company does not sell coffee. Only tea. It retained its full title when ownership changed and a new policy emerged simply to make things easier for its customers.

The resurgence of teas from mainland China—or the reemergence of teas from mainland China—into the world market has been a marked asset to the tea devotee's quest for the best. East India's shelves attest to the success of that goal, holding, among others, the lesser-known Young Hysons and Gunpowder teas.

East India's teas are sold in three-quarter-ounce samplers or in four-ounce packets, loose. Cost of the former is $.75, the latter, $2.50 each. Among its teas are Assam, Yunnan Black, Russian Caravan, Cashmir (yes, with a C this time), Oolong, Spicy Orange, San Francisco Blend and Wild Cherry.

India

R. N. AGARWALA & SON, NEHRU ROAD, DARJEELING

Flavorful teas with aroma and cup quality are produced in two parts of India, one of which is the high-elevation growing areas of Darjeeling. Agarwala & Son exports the finest grade of Orange Pekoe in half-, one- and two-kilogram packets. (One kilogram is equivalent to a little more than two pounds.)

To order, stipulate if the tea is to be sent by air or by sea mail (the latter will take forever). Approximate cost, including packing and surface postage, is 18.00 rupees (about $2.50) for one-half kilo of Darjeeling tea

Louisiana

FOX MOUNTAIN FARM, 1600 CHIPPEWA STREET, NEW ORLEANS 70130

In 1978, Fox Mountain's Voyce Durling-Jones and Teesta Valley Tea, Ltd.'s, director, Bharat Bajoria, signed an agreement which makes Fox Mountain the exclusive American importer of TVT's Darjeeling teas. (Between 55 and 75 percent of the Indian company's teas are sold to Poland and Russia.)

177

Tea by Mail

Teesta Valley lies seven thousand feet up in the foothills of the Himalayas and there, in the nineteenth century, the original "Old China" tea bushes were planted. In 1880, TVT won the first of several Gold Medals at the International Tea Exposition in Calcutta. The mother bushes are still being used and are still producing the quality tea, even though the crop yield per acre is small and the delicate leaf is expensive to harvest.

The cost of a tin of second flush, pure Darjeeling would be astronomical to produce, but a blend of rare Darjeeling from first, second and autumnal flushes is not. It is this blend which Ms. Durling-Jones selected after numerous samplings of tea over a year's time and days of intensive tea-tasting at the gardens. The Five Star quality blend was created to appeal to the American palate and purse. (Five Star Tea is the symbol for TGFOP —Top Grade Flowery Orange Pekoe, 1st Choice.)

All of Fox Mountain's black tea blends are sold in one-quarter-pound tins, each one bearing the seal of the Tea Board of India and containing a slip of paper authenticating the place of origin. Apparently, four times more Darjeeling teas appear on the market than is possible from the annual crop picked.

Fox Mountain's blends are for different times of the day. Morning Bed-Tea is from the gardens in Assam and Ms. Durling-Jones suggests serving it with warm milk. Three O'Clock Nilgiris is a flavory tea from the Blue Mountain tropics of southern India. It is equally good served hot or over ice. Dragonmoon is a blend of Darjeeling and Assam teas which is enjoyable any time of the day. Ms. Durling-Jones says it is particularly delicious when served with brandied fruit after dinner. The Rare Darjeeling, which should be taken without milk, is excellent in the late afternoon or late evening.

Prices upon request.

New York

MCNULTY'S TEA & COFFEE CO., INC., 109 CHRISTOPHER STREET, NEW YORK 10014

Stepping into McNulty's is stepping into the past, into a shop from another era. Indeed, McNulty's first opened in 1895 as a toy, almost, for a successful New York barrister. After several lives under different management, McNulty's truly came alive again in 1968 when former antique dealer, Bill Towart, became its owner. He sought out the best and offered the best and the freshest for sale—whether coffee or tea.

He also invented the one-ounce tea packet, providing a chance for customers to sample different teas, new teas, flavored teas, at a very modest price—about $.75 each—without having to settle for two, possibly three types in larger amounts.

Ask Mr. Towart how many different brands of tea he holds in his shop and he will tell you "at least eighty." The labels herald the specialties of Fortnum & Mason, Jacksons of Piccadilly, Twinings, Russian tea (called just that), teas from China, the domestic companies of Bigelow, Wagner and Boston, McNulty's own blends, and Gourmet Specialty Teas. The latter include Jamaican Ginger, Wild Cherry, Lime and Orange Mint, Spice and Gaucho's Delight.

Among the China teas, China Jasmine ("Really outstanding. My nose and taste tell me how Jasmine is blended and there is a hell of a difference between this and the synthetically blended."); Yunnan Black ("Very different, a unique type of flavor that is hard to describe but when you let someone smell its aroma, they buy it. It comes from a province noted for its black teas."); Lichee tea ("I thought they probably tossed in a few nuts. Actually, the lichee is one of the shade trees used in the tea gardens, and when it is in blossoms, its perfume is in the air. Full and heavy. And the tea leaves absorb it. When the tea is picked, it has a fine, winy aroma.").

Tea orders are mailed out the day they arrive. A brochure with current prices is free upon request.

GRACE TEA COMPANY LTD., 80 FIFTH AVENUE, NEW YORK 10003

Grace Tea was originally the gourmet arm of a leading tea importer. It is now a separate entity under new ownership but continues to provide its mail-order customers with the finest and the rarest of teas.

Under the heading The English Classics, Grace sells half-pound canisters of Super Darjeeling 6000; Formosa Oolong Supreme; Winey Keemun; Lapsang Souchong, Smoky No. 1; and Before the Rain Jasmine. The same five are also contained in a sample gift package of two-ounce tasters, while the Gourmet Trio holds Formosa Oolong Supreme, Winey Keemun and Before the Rain Jasmine in three half-pound tins.

What are they like?

Superb Darjeeling 6000 is specially picked from the early summer flush and hard to come by.

Formosa Oolong Supreme is considered the champagne of teas and personal choice of professional tea tasters. It is hand-picked only once annually.

Winey Keemun is fine for breakfast, strong with a smooth winey flavor.

Lapsang Souchong, Smoky No. 1 is the best of the smoky teas.

Before the Rain Jasmine is picked in spring, blended with summer flowers, light and fragrant.

Grace's brochure and price list, sent upon request, also feature Grace Connoisseur Blend; Fancy Ceylon, a blend of the premier grades from the Ouvah and Nuwara Eliya districts; Gunpowder Pearl, which Grace admits is not the lightest of teas but is a cherished green tea; Pure Assam, back-

bone of the tea blenders' trade; and The Original Earl Grey Mixture, which
Grace is quick to point out is "not a corrupt version of this fine blend, but
the original Superb black teas."

179

*Tea
by Mail*

Virginia

FIRST COLONY COFFEE & TEA COMPANY, INC., 204-222 WEST 22
STREET, P.O.B. 11005 (MAIL ORDER DEPT.), NORFOLK 23517

First Colony is a young company—incorporated in 1977—but it is an off-
shoot of a long-established company in wholesale tea and coffee (the James
G. Gill Company). First Colony deals only in specialized teas and, to be
fair, specialized coffees.

Asked to define the greatest characteristic of the company, its president,
J. Gill Brockenbrough, Jr., said: "Our main strength has been in China teas
since 1972, when this market opened up again. We have brought in some
teas from China that the United States has not had before."

The spectrum of China teas is very broad, surpassing every other tea
nation, according to Brockenbrough. His company carries about twenty
different China teas and maintains standard controls on approximately sixty
different teas. But, with China teas, Brockenbrough merely reorders by lot
number. "I never have to sample a tea of theirs again once I have tasted
it the first time. They always maintain that same standard. All other teas
I buy I sample, again and again, year after year."

First Colony's teas are sold in quarter-, half- and one-pound weights,
packed loose in tin caddies decorated with tea chests and clipper ships.
Among the China teas: Keemun Mandarin (First Colony terms it "one of
the world's finest"); Dragon Well, the legendary green tea of Chekiang
and among the best; Cloud Mist, a rare and fabled tea from Old China;
Pinhead Gunpowder, a special green, extra-grade tea especially imported by
First Colony; Young Hyson, a delicate green; and Pingsuey, called "a
stylish green tea from the seaboard region."

The India teas number Gold Tip Darjeeling, Darjeeling and Assam. From
Sri Lanka: Ramboda Orange Pekoe, a very good Ceylon Black; and Dibula
Orange Pekoe, very, very fine.

Traditional blends include Earl Grey, English Breakfast and Queens
Blend (the latter originated by James G. Gill in 1876).

Also on the list of teas are the Mainland China Tea Bricks, ornate tablets
of compressed tea. First mention of tea bricks came during the Sung dynasty
and for hundreds of years these tablets were prized by Chinese emperors,
Russian czars, and anyone else fortunate enough to own one. The tablets
were carried by merchants on their travels to Tibet where they were used
as currency in trading.

The molds used to form the bricks are centuries old, their "faces" carrying many traditional Oriental symbols and images of life-styles. The most
aesthetically pleasing weighs two and a half pounds and costs $16.00. First
Colony has been selling them since 1975. Prices on request.

NORTHWESTERN COFFEE MILLS, 217 NORTH BROADWAY, MILWAUKEE 53202

Northwestern was the city's first coffee merchant but soon added tea and has kept tea in the forefront ever since. The teas are imported by the chest and blended before being shipped, sold in quarter- to one-pound amounts of loose tea. Among the flavors, Russian Caravan; Star Anise Blend; Darjeeling; Second Flush; Backsettler Blend (which Northwestern claims fits nearly all tea-drinking occasions and is forgiving of brewing mistakes); Cinnamon and Mint.

Prices range from $1.50 to $1.95 for a quarter pound to $3.70 to $5.40 for one pound. Postage is a flat $2.50 on any order.

England

FORTNUM & MASON LTD., PICCADILLY, LONDON W1A 1ER

The partnership between William Fortnum and Hugh Mason began in 1707 but it took two generations more before London was aware of their shop's existence. By 1761, with the help of royal court contacts, Fortnum & Mason became synonymous with the choicest of foods and importing of fine teas and spices from the East.

Their first "mail-order" requests came during the Napoleonic Wars when F&M found itself inundated with desperate appeals from Wellington's hungry officers. The demands were met and, one might say, set the standard for much of the company's future trade in catering to those in need of sustenance at all times and in all places—provided, of course, they could pay for it.

In 1854 came the Crimean War and once again Fortnum stepped in to feed not only the privileged officers but to succor the many sick. From Queen Victoria came an order to dispatch to Miss Florence Nightingale a huge consignment of beef tea. World War I found Fortnum prepared to meet almost every demand made upon them from British Forces round the world, action that was repeated a short thirty years later.

F&M teas are sold in the usual packaging—and in the more decorative. A Mason's Ironstone jar embossed with the company's clock design may hold a half or one pound of its royal blend tea, while tin caddies harbor a selection of teas in various weights. A particularly delightful form of tea "packaging" is a French Limoges teapot filled with half a pound of a selected tea. It is a good thought to keep in mind for holiday time. Prices from F&M upon request.

TPIC has specialized in blending fine teas for overseas connoisseurs for more than half a century. Specially selected, specially blended and free of scent, the teas brew well in all kinds of water. There are six selections to round out the twenty-four hours of a day—Morning Tea, Lunchtime Tea, Afternoon Tea, After-Dinner Tea, Evening Tea and Drawing Room Tea. A trial parcel containing four of the six blends can be bought or they can be ordered individually, loose and packed in tin caddies.

Sri Lanka

THE CEYLON TEA PROMOTION BOARD, P.O.B. 295, COLOMBO

As mentioned earlier, it took the coffee disaster in the mid-1800s to switch Sri Lanka (then Ceylon) to tea. Ceylon teas have been used in blends for a long time, but the Tea Board has been promoting its pure teas in gift packs. The "Five Fine Ceylon Teas," net weight one and a quarter pounds a package, contain teas from Kandy, Nuwara Eliya, Dimbula and Ruhuna. The Tea Board is very quick to answer any request and quote prices. If a gift pack is not sufficient, individual tins and foil packets of tea can be ordered.

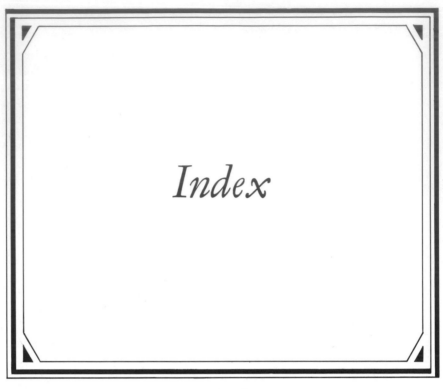

Index